Ad
Change-mapping

Exploring, resolving and addressing issues of any size and complexity

Tom Graves with Joseph Chittenden

Published by
Tetradian Books
www.tetradian.com/books
info@tetradian.com

First published June 2022
ISBN 978-1-906681-44-9 (Paperback)
ISBN 978-1-906681-45-6 (Ebook)
First Edition

Legal disclaimer

Advanced
Change-mapping

Exploring, resolving and addressing issues of
any size and complexity

Tom Graves with Joseph Chittenden

Contents

Part 1: How to explore complex issues

Part 2: How to get more from Linked Missions

Part 3: How to ask the right questions

Part 4: What have you learnt?

Preface
Tackling large and complex issues

How do you tackle a truly immense and complex issue?
This has been the concern of the author for over thirty years.
He found that many people, while comfortable in their own
disciplines, have struggled if they encountered a different
context. They would try to force fit what worked for them in
different situations, with at best mixed results.
He developed a system called *Five Elements* which allowed
the user to work in any context. While *Five Elements* achieved
the author's aims, it was quite difficult for non Enterprise
Architects to pick up. *Change-mapping* took the underlying
Five Elements methods and presented a simple system that
could be used for any issue in any context.
While this book explores large and complex issues, it works
exactly the same way as described in the first two books.
As with those the principal aim is to gather ideas, insights and
information and be able to get that information in any form to
those that need it, when they need it.

Tom Graves
Bendigo, Australia
June 2022

A big thank you!
To our co-creators and valued patrons

This book would not have existed without all of the people who over the years have helped to bring *Change-mapping* to a wider audience.

The author would like to thank, amongst others:
Michael Smith (Mexico)
Helena Read (Australia)
Bard Papegaaij (Netherlands)
Eric Weinstein (USA)
Nate Gerber (Canada)

Patrons
The author would also like to thank all the valued Patrons at *www.patreon.com/tetradian* who helped fund the production of this book.
They have also given excellent feedback and helped with testing the materials.

How you can get involved!
To find out more about Change-mapping visit:
www. changemappingbook.com

If you would like to be involved with the development of new tools, testing and more then head over to Patreon to get involved.
www.patreon.com/ tetradian

About the author
Tom Graves

Tom is known as a highly innovative thought leader on the futures of business. With a keen eye for systems and structure, he has nearly 40 years experience in knowledge management, skills research and software development.
He is a prolific author, and experienced presenter on radio and television, at conferences and in workshops and seminars.
Contact: info@tetradian.com

About the designer
Joseph Chittenden

Joseph has produced concepts and visuals for companies such as: *Tesco, Lotus sports cars, T-Mobile, Honda, Makita, UK Cabinet Office, Superdrug/3Phones,* and others on behalf of design agencies in England and Dubai.
Contact: visuals@jc3dvis.co.uk

What is *Change-mapping*?

A quick overview

The first two *Change-mapping* books

Inside the first book: *Change-mapping*, you learn how to run small *Change-mapping* missions, see it in action and avoid common problems. There is also a complete set of basic tools to help you learn how to use *Change-mapping*. It is available on Amazon and other book retailers. **ISBN** 978-1906681401

The second book: ***Tools for Change-mapping*** introduces a set of detailed tools to help you explore, resolve and address issues of any size and complexity It is available on Amazon and other book retailers. **ISBN** 978-1906681425

This book is the follow-on to the previous *Change-mapping* books *(see left)*. We recommend that you read those books before reading this one.

What happens if you have an issue which needs to be resolved? A typical response is to plan how to resolve the issue and then resolve it. While this is fine in principle, it can miss out vital steps, such as *'Why does the issue need solving?'* or *'Is this the best way to resolve the issue?'* Change-mapping is used to answer these types of questions. It does this by using a simple map system which breaks down any issue into manageable parts, as shown below.

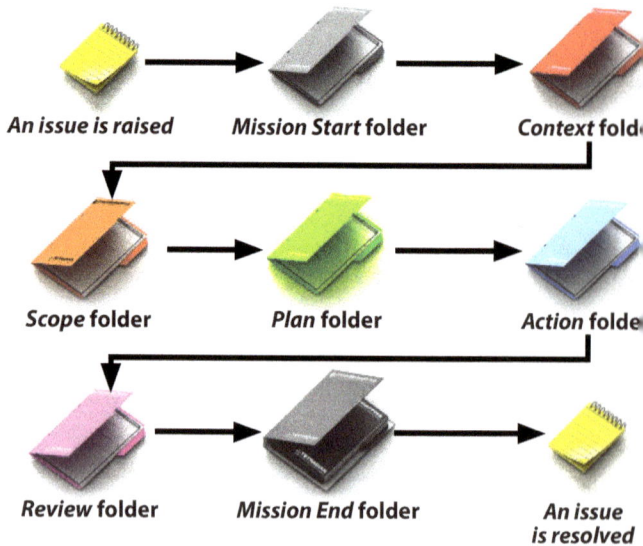

An issue is raised	**Mission Start** folder	**Context** folder
Scope folder	**Plan** folder	**Action** folder
Review folder	**Mission End** folder	*An issue is resolved*

All these parts make up a ***mission*** to explore or resolve an issue. Every ***mission*** is run by a small team of ***Explorers***, who are assisted by a ***Pathfinder*** who keeps the mission on track and an ***Observer*** who records all that is found.

When running a ***mission*** the team use tools to gather ideas, information and insights. How the tools work is discussed on the next page.

What is a *Change-mapping* mission?
Exploring, resolving and addressing an issue

Within the first *Change-mapping* book were a set of basic tools which were deliberately simplified, so that you would not be daunted when first learning how to use them. Using these tools was done using missions.

In the first book a mission was seen as finished when the folders *(see left)* were all completed.

In this book we show how to link missions, allowing you to explore, address or resolve large and complex issues in more detail. Linked missions are made up of a set of missions. For example we show in the first part of this book a Linked Mission made up of 13 missions.

Each mission has folders inside it just like in a single mission *(see left)*. Inside each folder are tool-sheets such as the one shown below.

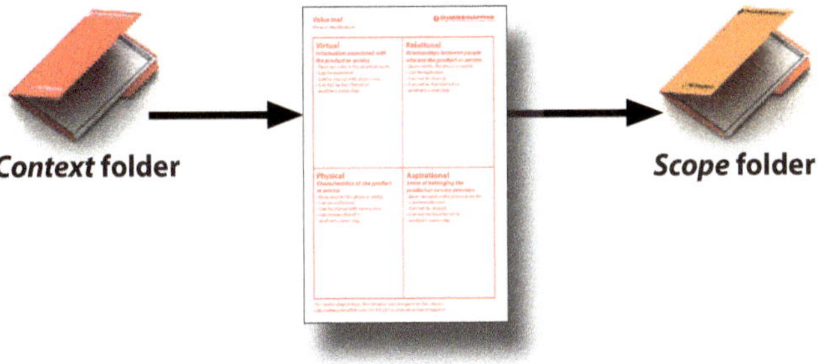

Context folder   **Scope** folder

What is an enterprise?
The word 'enterprise' is mentioned throughout this book.
An organisation is part of an enterprise but it is not the enterprise.
If we imagine a city council, their enterprise is to run the city for all stakeholders. Running the city involves a huge amount of individual issues which need to be resolved.
This continual resolving of issues is the enterprise. Inside the enterprise will be the organisation, suppliers, customers, equipment and much more.
For more information see www.slideshare.net/ tetradian/the-enterprise-is- the-story/

Scenarios allow you to see how each mission inside the Linked Mission would typically be used.

For example the *Far Future* mission is shown on page 36, exploring the ramifications of updating an Enterprise Resource Planning system.

Note though that *any* mission can be used within *any* scenario. For example the *Far Future* mission could be used to explore the ramifications of making a city more sustainable *(see page 36)*.

So read through the scenarios to see what the missions and their associated tools are used for and then use them in your missions!

See page 4 to find out more about Linked Missions.

What is a *Change-mapping* tool?

Gathering ideas, information and insights

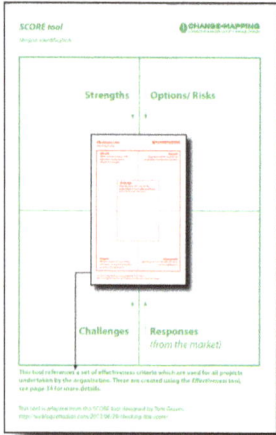

A sample tool-sheet
*Here is an example of a typical Change-mapping tool. This is the **SCORE** tool (see Book 2, page 74). This tool has five sections to be answered by the **Explorers***. The **Observer*** would actually write down what the Explorers find out. This then becomes a record of what was found and is kept inside the folder. Each tool is associated with a particular folder, for example this tool is used in the **Plan** Folder**

*See page iii

As mentioned on the previous page, *Change-mapping* uses missions which contain folders, which themselves contain tools. The tools shown in all these books are paper-based tool-sheets designed to pose questions. They are not meant to supply answers, as logically it is impossible to provide answers for every possible issue. They work with the **Explorers** *(see page iii)* trying to answer the questions posed on the tool-sheets. Book 1 introduced some very simple tools, while Book 2 expanded the tool-set with more detailed tools. This book also describes some new tools, which are described in detail in this book *(see right)*.

One of the key points of *Change-mapping* is that tools are connected so that people can see where they are used and if they have been filled in. When you are running a simple single mission it should be easy to store and share the tool-sheets and what was written on them. But when you tackle large and complex issues, potentially thousands of tool-sheets could be needed. Then a more dedicated method of storing, tracking and sharing the tool-sheets is required. And why we used a particular tool.

This is discussed in the **Library** section *(see page 64)*.
The tools described here are paper-based, but really anything could be used as a tool, such as a PEST tool or an interview or a physical prototype. Therefore when we mention gathering information, we mean in any form.

Downloading the new tools
Using the tools for your missions

You can download blank versions of the Red tool-sheets used in the Linked Missions *(such as the one below)* at: **www.changemappingbook.com/advanced-change-mapping-book**

A list of the new tools
While this and the other books focus on Tetradian tools which have been designed to work with Change-mapping, there is nothing stopping you using other tools to get the information you need. You will see in Book 2, page 106 a diagram showing a sample list of tools and how you could add them to your missions. Many of the pages in this book also list useful tools and when to use them inside Linked Missions.

Review mission tool   **CHANGE-MAPPING**
Mission identification:

Mission 12 of 13 Answer all questions using Change-mapping techniques (Book 1, page 18).

How long after the issue is resolved will the review take place?

Was the issue successfully resolved?

Was the plan effective or did you have to adapt the plan?

Did you stay true to the enterprise's and organisation's vision and values?

How might the enactment change if it was scaled up?

What would we do differently if the enactment was repeated?

Have stakeholders embraced the change brought about by the issue's resolution?

How did the equipment, materials and location perform during the enactment?

How did the people involved with the enactment perform?

Was there enough time, money and information available for the enactment

Download a blank copy at: www.changemappingbook.com/advanced-change-mapping-book

Part 1:
How to explore complex issues

In this part of the book we look at how to explore,
resolve or address large complex issues.
In *Change-mapping* this is done
using **Linked Missions**.
We show this with two examples, a city trying to be
more sustainable and a legal firm updating their
Enterprise Resource Planning systems.

What is a Linked Mission?
Exploring, resolving or addressing a complex issue

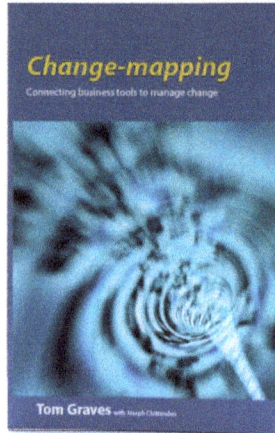

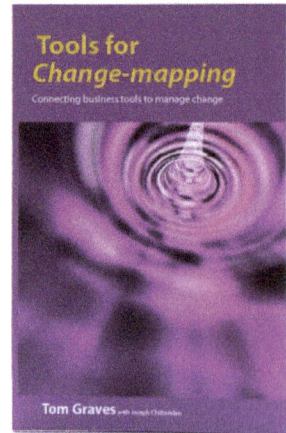

Tackling an issue
In Change-mapping we explore an issue to see if we might want to change it. We might also resolve an issue. Finally we can address an issue where we continuously resolve it. In this book we will use the word **tackle** *which covers: exploring, resolving or addressing an issue.*

An overview
In the first two *Change-mapping* books *(see above)* we described a system to explore project level issues.
But when you need to explore much larger issues, which may take place in different countries and take years to address, then a **Linked Mission** would be used. A Linked Mission works in the same way as a normal mission, except that each mission is linked and tackles a specific part of the issue.
Each mission has a status dot: green for complete, orange for in-progress, red for incomplete and black for archived.
In addition each mission has black arrows showing that you work your way down, but that you can also loop back.
There are also pink arrows which show the flow of information through the main Library *(see page 64)* and your Linked Mission. Inside each mission you will use tools which are described in the following pages.

How does a Linked Mission compare to project management?
Projects are familiar to everyone as an approach to exploring, resolving or addressing issues. *Change-mapping* aligns with many of the stages of project management.
The diagram on the far right shows the typical stages *(the blue text)* of a project and how they align with a typical *Change-mapping* Linked Mission. At first sight the typical project seems simpler, but it *can* gloss over vital parts that allow an issue to be explored, resolved or addressed effectively.

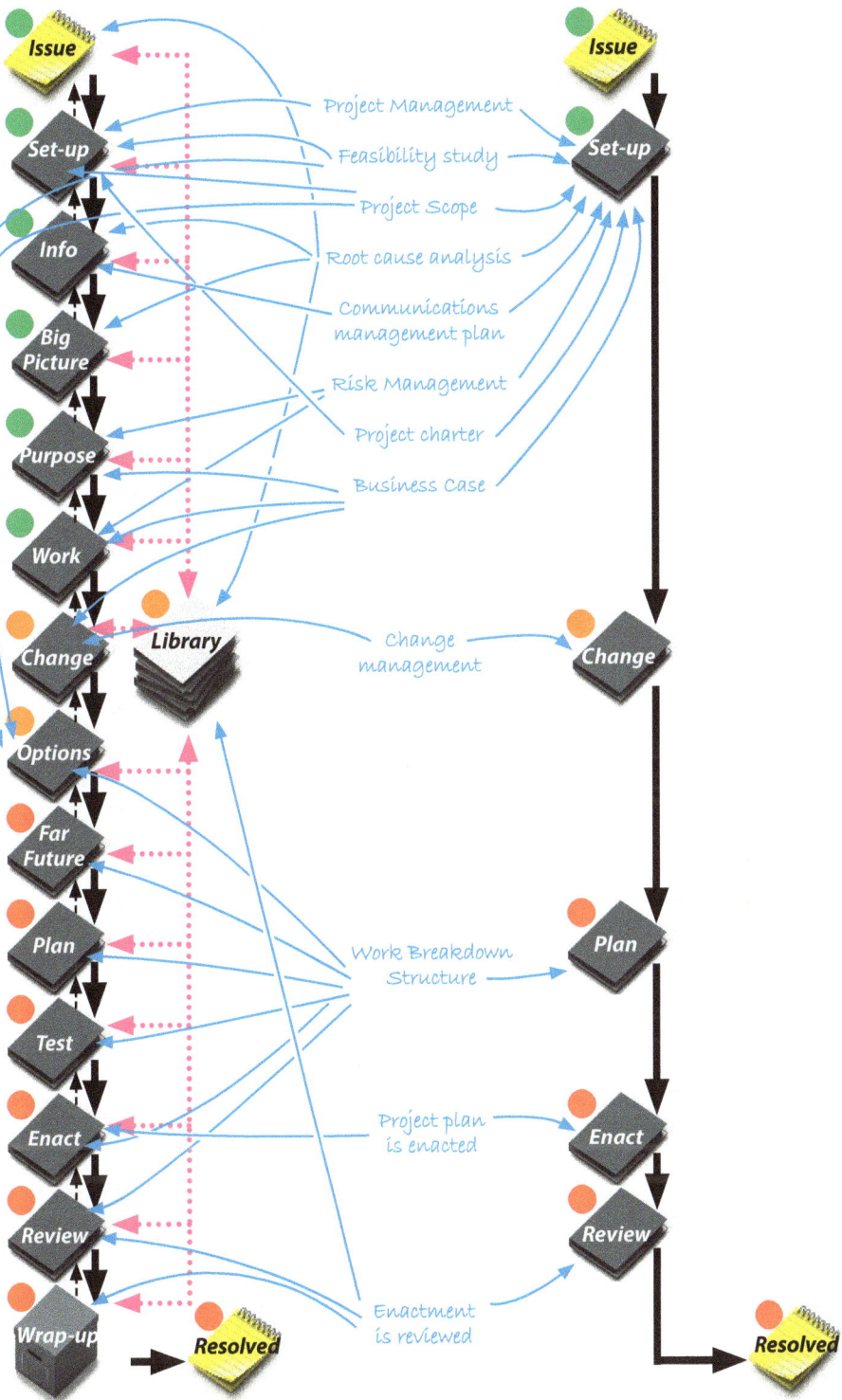

Diagram showing a typical
Linked Mission

Diagram showing a typical project

An issue is raised

An issue needs to be explored, resolved or addressed

In brief

In this part of the Linked Mission an issue is raised. Here we establish what the issue is. For example, a city council raises the issue that they want the city to be more sustainable.

What is the issue?

Often when an issue is raised there can be a rush to resolve that issue. In that rush, assumptions can be made which can sometimes prove incorrect. Often to try to remove risk, various tools are used to build up a picture of what is happening. This again can cause problems as the tools are not connected, giving fragments of information.

The Linked Mission helps to give a simple, adaptable framework to tackle any issue of any size and complexity. The first stage of a Linked Mission is to raise an issue and define that issue, which is described on the following pages.

Worked example

A legal firm in Melbourne, Australia uses ERP to help manage people and assets within their organisation.

The COO has received reports that their current ERP solution is struggling since the opening of the new office in London. At the next board meeting the COO raises the issue of the need to update the organisation's ERP. The COO states his reasons for updating the ERP. With such a potential transformation of the organisation, the board expresses caution.

After the meeting the COO assembles the Strategy team. "How can we update our ERP, is the issue I have raised".

The strategy team ask for a overview of the issue.

Based on the answers to these questions, they feel that for such a large and complex issue a Linked Mission could help.

Raising the issue

In our example the strategy team ask the COO for an overview of the issue. They need to work out what the issue is and if it needs to be explored, resolved or addressed.

To help them decide this they use the Sense-making tool (Book 2, page 10) to obtain general information about the issue. After using the tool they see that the issue will involve a large amount of exploration. They decide to use a Linked Mission to break down the complex issue into smaller parts. They have used the tool as part of an informal briefing, before the Linked Mission was started.

Sense-making tool

⬤ CHANGE-MAPPING

Mission Identification:

What is the issue?	When is it thought the issue occurs or occurred?	Where is it thought the issue occurs or occurred?
How is it thought the issue occurs or occurred?	Who is thought to be affected by the issue occurring?	What is it thought to cause the issue occurring?
Why does the issue need resolving?	What apart from people is thought to be affected when the issue occurs?	Why is it thought the issue occurs?

Statement about the issue:

This tool is adapted from a blog by Tom Graves:
http://weblog.tetradian.com/2018/03/14/sensemaking-into-the-void/

Issue

Set up

Info

Big Picture

Purpose

Work

Library

Change

Options

Far Future

Plan

Test

Enact

Review

Wrap-up

Resolved

Diagram showing the start of a Linked Mission

The *Set up* mission
Setting up a Linked Mission

In brief

In this part of the Linked Mission we explore how we will explore the issue raised. For example, how would a city council explore the issue of how to have a more sustainable city.

Setting up a Linked Mission

If we need to tackle a large and complex issue, **how** we tackle the issue will need to be worked out.

This mission is used to work out who will be doing what in each of the following missions. For example, who will be involved with the **Test mission** (see diagram on the right). What resources, people and time will be required? Exploring all of these aspects of the entire Linked Mission allows forward planning and avoids bias in certain areas. Once you have all of the above examined, you should have everything in place to explore and resolve your issue.

Worked example

In our example the strategy team approach the PMO to help with planning how the Linked Mission will be run.

Both teams use this mission to break down the issue. They start to break down how long will exploring the issue take and what budgets are involved.

If this exploration confirms updating the ERP will indeed benefit the firm, then they will start planning the actual update. This would include the skills, people and equipment needed to enact the change.

Working out all of the above will take time and so the two teams are allotted two weeks to produce an initial schedule. This schedule is put to the board for approval. In this way each mission within the Linked Mission acts as a gateway. Allowing the board to have clear gateways at which they can pull the plug, rather than initiating an ERP system update that might not even be needed.

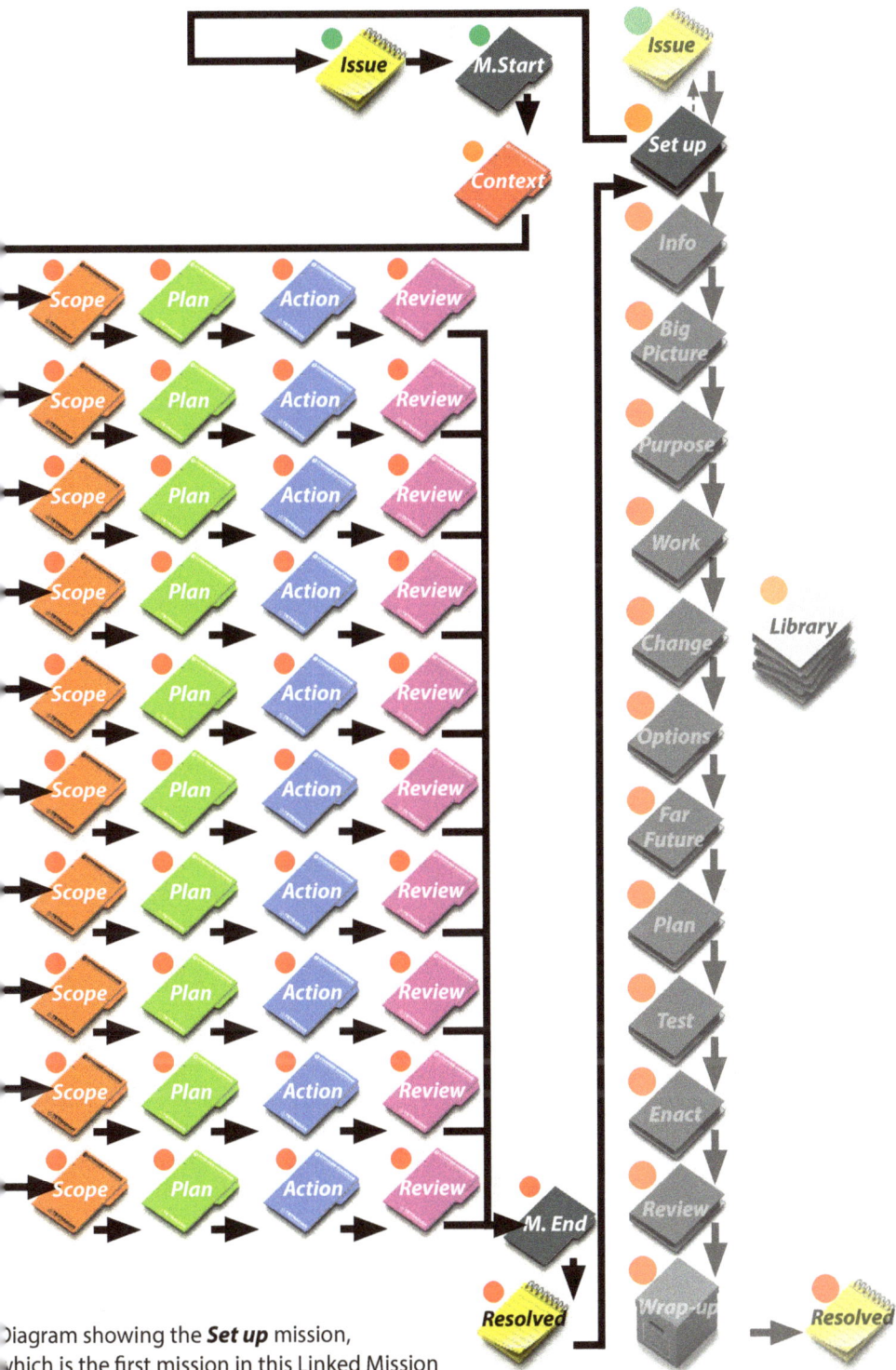

Diagram showing the **Set up** mission,
which is the first mission in this Linked Mission

Using non-Change-mapping tools in this mission

- Project management tools
- Feasibility study
- Project Scope document
- Project Charter
- RACI
- PRINCE2

These tools could be used alongside the questions shown on the right.

How to use this mission

How can this mission help you?
This mission is used to set up the Linked Mission itself. It describes who will be doing what and what you want to achieve, such as resolving an issue.

What needs to be done before using this mission tool?
Ideally before the mission starts you will have a detailed description of what the issue is and other information such as that shown on the tool *(see right)*. This would be gathered in the **An issue is raised** stage *(see page 6)* which acts like a pre-mission briefing.

Who is typically involved in this mission?
Project managers, Programme managers, Portfolio managers Vice-presidents, IT Change leads.

Warning signs while running the mission
- Rushing to start the Linked Mission without considering how the Linked Mission will be conducted.
- Not having a clear picture of what the issue is.
- Resolving or addressing the issue without first exploring the issue.
- Not having a clear picture of what you want to achieve.
- Rushing to the plan mission.
- Analysis-paralysis
- Poor leadership and decision-making.

What works well with this mission?
Γ Detailed notes from the issue raiser, see page 6.

Δ The **Holomap** tool for defining who does what, when resolving an issue *(Book 2, Page 22)*.

Θ The **Where to start** tool for idea generation while resolving issues. *(Book 2, Page 78)*.

Λ The **Decision** tool for reviewing decision making *(Book 2, Page 44)*.

Σ The **Basic Context tools 2/3/4** for specifying what you want to achieve *(Book 1, Page 72)*.

Φ You will need to refer to the **Big Picture Mission** *(page 16)*, the **Purpose Mission** *(page 20)* and the **Work Mission** *(page 24)* to cross-check that resolving the issue aligns with the values set in those missions.

Set up mission tool

Mission identification: Linked Mission to update our Legal firm's ERP system
2OCTOBER2032-MISSION-02048

Mission 1 of 13 *Answer all questions using Change-mapping techniques (Book 1, page 18).*

Why is the issue to be explored, resolved or addressed?   **Γ**
The COO has called for the ERP system to be updated in response to calls
from various stakeholders.

When is the issue to be explored, resolved or addressed?   **Θ**
Ideally we will take a month to explore the issue. If that exploration shows we
should proceed with the update then will continue the Linked Mission with the
aim of resolving the issue. Meaning we will have updated the ERP system.

What is the issue to be explored, resolved or addressed?   **Γ** **Θ**
The COO believes the ERP system should be updated to the latest version.

Who will explore, resolve or address the issue?   **Δ** **Θ**
We (the strategy team) need to discuss with the PMO who will first explore
the issue. A different set of people will be involved if our legal firm decide to
update the ERP system.

Where is the issue to be explored, resolved or addressed?   **Θ**
The issue will be explored in our legal firm. Most likely the resolution (if it
happens) may take place in a virtual environment before being tested in a
small scale staggered roll-out.

What equipment/info is needed to explore, resolve or address the issue?   **Θ**
We most likely will need a NESTED MISSION (Book 1, page 114) to see
what we will need. For exploration mostly info gathering and interviews.
The IT dept will specify what equipment they would need for a roll-out.

How will decisions be made during the Linked Mission?   **Λ**
We will use each mission inside the Linked Mission as a gateway for
decision making. But we also need to avoid rushed, uninformed decisions.

What would happen if the issue was not explored, resolved or addressed?   **Φ**
The missions will confirm this, but at a guess either we will carry on as
before or we will be less adaptable to changing circumstances.

What would a successful outcome of the Linked Mission look like?   **Σ** **Φ**
If we knew that updating the ERP was in our best interest and then that the
update was done as smoothly as possible (INSIGHT A trade-offs tool,
would be useful here. For example time versus money).

Which standards, regulations and laws do you need to be aware of?   **Φ**
We will need this information before a resolution took place, I imagine that
we would get this info in the following missions and then come back to this
mission and fill in this section.

The *Info* mission
Gathering all relevant information

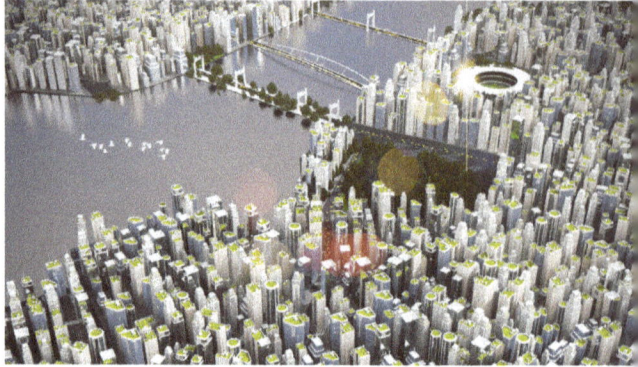

In brief

In this part of the Linked Mission we establish how any information* that we find will be shared and stored.

For example, how would a city council store and share all the information they find while exploring how to make the city more sustainable.

*Information such as data, physical prototypes and more.

Is there any available information?

For *Change-mapping* to be effective you will need a Library of information. Part of that information will be generated inside your Linked Mission and part will be gathered from outside the Linked Mission. This mission is used to setup how all that information is stored and shared, so that all that need it, can access it. The information you gather will help your Linked Mission and may also be useful to people running different Linked Missions. The Library allows that sharing of up-to date information. The main Library is discussed further on page 64.

Worked example

In our legal firm example, they have a main Library which handles all legal documents, financial records and so on. Inside this Library there is a section dedicated to Change-mapping.* In our mission the team make contact with the Library to inform of their needs and to ask if they have any useful information which could be used in the ERP issue.

The Linked Mission itself has its own mission Library which is used to share information inside and outside the mission. The strategy team who are running the Linked Mission will stay in regular contact with the main Library.

This will allow them to keep updated on other teams working on similar issues and to share what they have found with other teams.

*Our Library keeps information from Linked Missions run by other teams exploring other issues. Because information found in other Linked Missions may be useful to us.

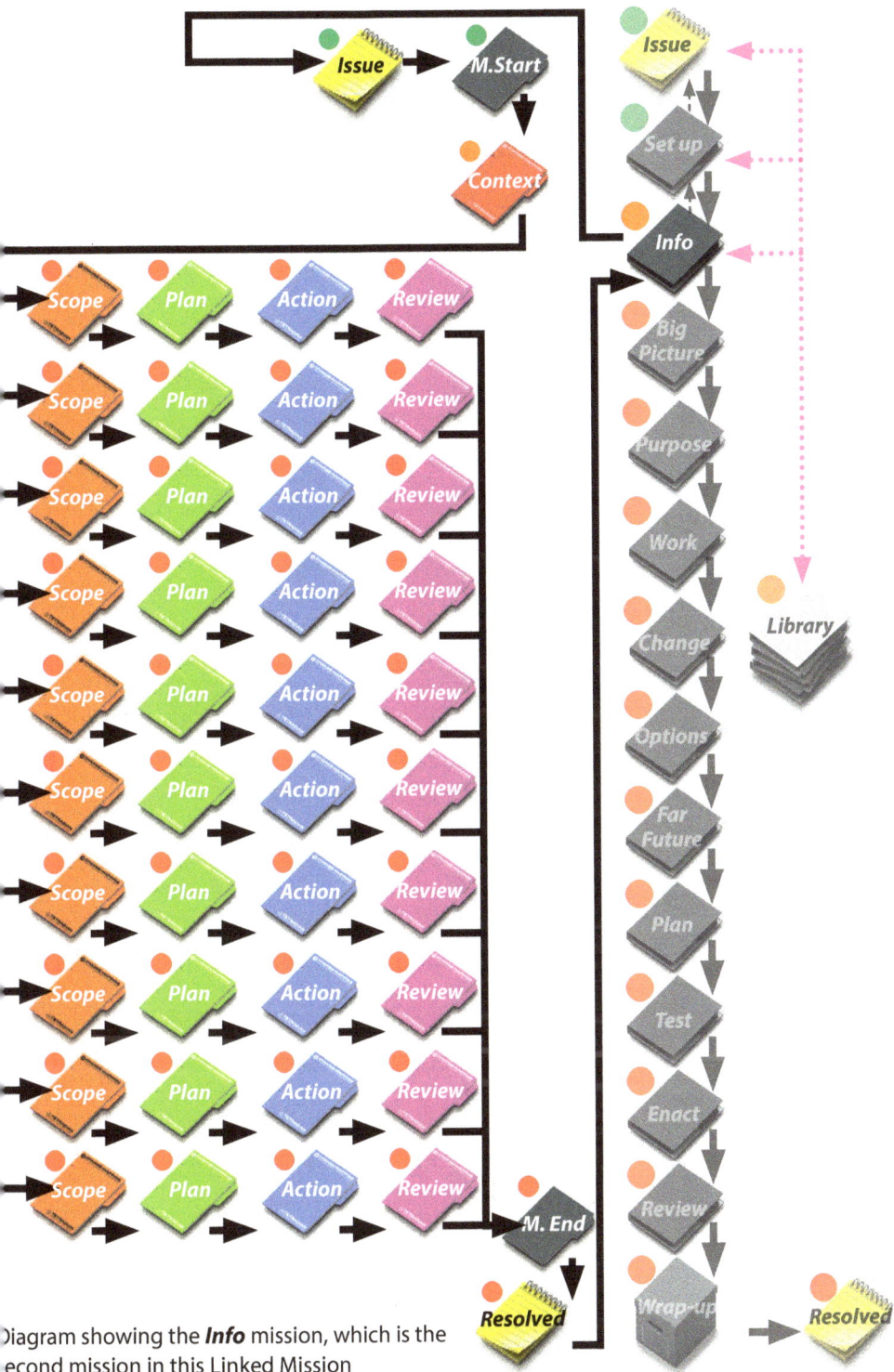

Diagram showing the **Info** mission, which is the second mission in this Linked Mission

Using non-Change-mapping tools in this mission

• *Communications management plan*
• *RACI*
• *Change control*
• *Changelog*
• *Disaster recovery plan*
• *Data migration*
• *Tools to set standards for saving, categorising and distributing information.*
• *Tools to set standards for archiving, deleting and securing information.*
• *Tools to set standards for updating, recreating and migrating information.*
These tools could be used alongside the questions shown on the right.
Therefore the information here will set up effective information-sharing while running a Linked Mission.

How to use this mission

How can this mission help you?

This mission is used to establish what information will be stored and shared within the entire Linked Mission.
This will help to keep your information focused and relevant for all of those involved.

What needs to be done before using this mission tool?

Change-mapping shares all kinds of information. How this information is shared and stored needs to be addressed. Ideally your organisation will have a main Library with easy- to-use standards. You will then be able to contact the Library to make sure that you have all you need from them and if you have any special requirements from the Library. If you don't have a main Library, see page 64.

Who is typically involved in this mission?

Project, Programme, Portfolio and Organisation based record-keepers. For example, accounts keeping financial records.

Warning signs while running the mission

• Rushing to start the Linked Mission without considering how information will be stored and shared.
• Not recording information during missions. The Observer *(Book 1, page 12)* must focus on capturing information.
• Conversely, recording every single piece of information, even that which is not relevant to the Linked Mission.

What works well with this mission?

Λ The **Effectiveness tool** *(Book 2, page 34)* to set standards for effectiveness in sharing and storing information.

Ξ The **Holomap tool** *(Book 2, page 22)* to explore who are the stakeholders in information sharing and storage.

Σ The **Value tool** *(Book 2, page 6)* to explore what types of information needs to be saved and why.

CHANGE→MAPPING
CONNECTING BUSINESS TOOLS TO MANAGE CHANGE

Mission identification: Linked Mission to update our Legal firm's ERP system
20OCTOBER2032-MISSION-02048

Mission 2 of 13 Answer all questions using Change-mapping techniques (Book 1, page 18).

How will your Change-mapping information be saved?
We are exploring about a potential ERP system update. Most of our
information should be written notes, discussions and internet articles.
We will keep hand-written tool-sheets (such as this one and PDFs)

How will your Change-mapping information be categorised?
The main focus of the mission will be ERP. So we need information from
the Library with this focus. We will use tags including: ERP, IT, Enterprise-
resource-management.

How will your Change-mapping information be distributed?
We will have a shared drive on our internal server, where all team members
can access the information. After each Change-mapping session it will be
uploaded to the drive for others to access.

How will your Change-mapping information be updated?
At the end of each Change-mapping session, all information will be uploaded
to the main Library. We will use the Library's standards for revisions.

How will your Change-mapping information be archived?
We need to archive our Linked Mission information using the standard
Library archiving methods, as if we ever do a new update, we will need to see
what we did in this update.

How will your Change-mapping information be deleted?
We feel that the mission lead will have the final say, but as a rough estimate
7 years we will keep records for the mission.

How will your Change-mapping information be secured?
Our organisation secures all its information using standard encryption,
back-ups and anti-virus. Physical information will be kept in the Library in
a physical Change-mapping box.

How will your Change-mapping information be recreated?
Our Library has back-up systems and disaster recovery plans to try
and reduce the effects of lost data. Physical items (INSIGHT we need to
investigate how these would be recreated. Tacit information, we would need to
record it before staff left for example).

How will your Change-mapping information be migrated?
Our Library has a data migration strategy in place, which we follow.
Migrating physical objects might involve 3D scanning the objects and
storing them digitally.

Does your Linked Mission have any special requirements from the Library?
We may need to do testing of uploading an updated ERP, we need to find out
how we can store those tests. Is there a way to video screen-grabs which we can
keep as part of our records. (Spoke to Library, plenty of simple methods to
screen capture processes).

Λ ☰ Σ

The *Big Picture* mission
Understanding the context of your issue

In brief

In this part of the Linked Mission we explore what is the enterprise (or story) we are part of and how the issue raised relates to the enterprise. For example, how does making the city more sustainable fit into the story of the city, its inhabitants and beyond?

Building good foundations

At first this mission can seem a luxury, surely we know the enterprise we are part of. There can be confusion about what an enterprise even is *(see page 68)*.

This mission uses information mostly gathered from other sources to cross-check that the issue you want to resolve, actually needs resolving. This mission presents the *Big Picture* and what is valued within that space. If what you plan to resolve doesn't support that enterprise, then problems are likely to crop up later on. It's a bit like building a new house starting from the roof, before building the foundations...

Worked example

In our example the strategy team need to find out how to update the ERP. Initially they feel they don't need to know about the industry they are in. "That's just our organisation, isn't it?" They ask the main Library to provide information about the enterprise. They find that their organisation is only part of the enterprise (see page 66). And that the issue needs to support the overall enterprise, otherwise why do it?

Using the information from the Main Library they start to look at the Big Picture, which shows an increasing demand for real time information at any location. Updating the ERP would facilitate sharing of real time information.

If the big picture had shown the opposite, then pushing ahead with a costly update would have led to an urgent examination of how to proceed. But in our example, they decided to proceed to the next mission: Purpose.

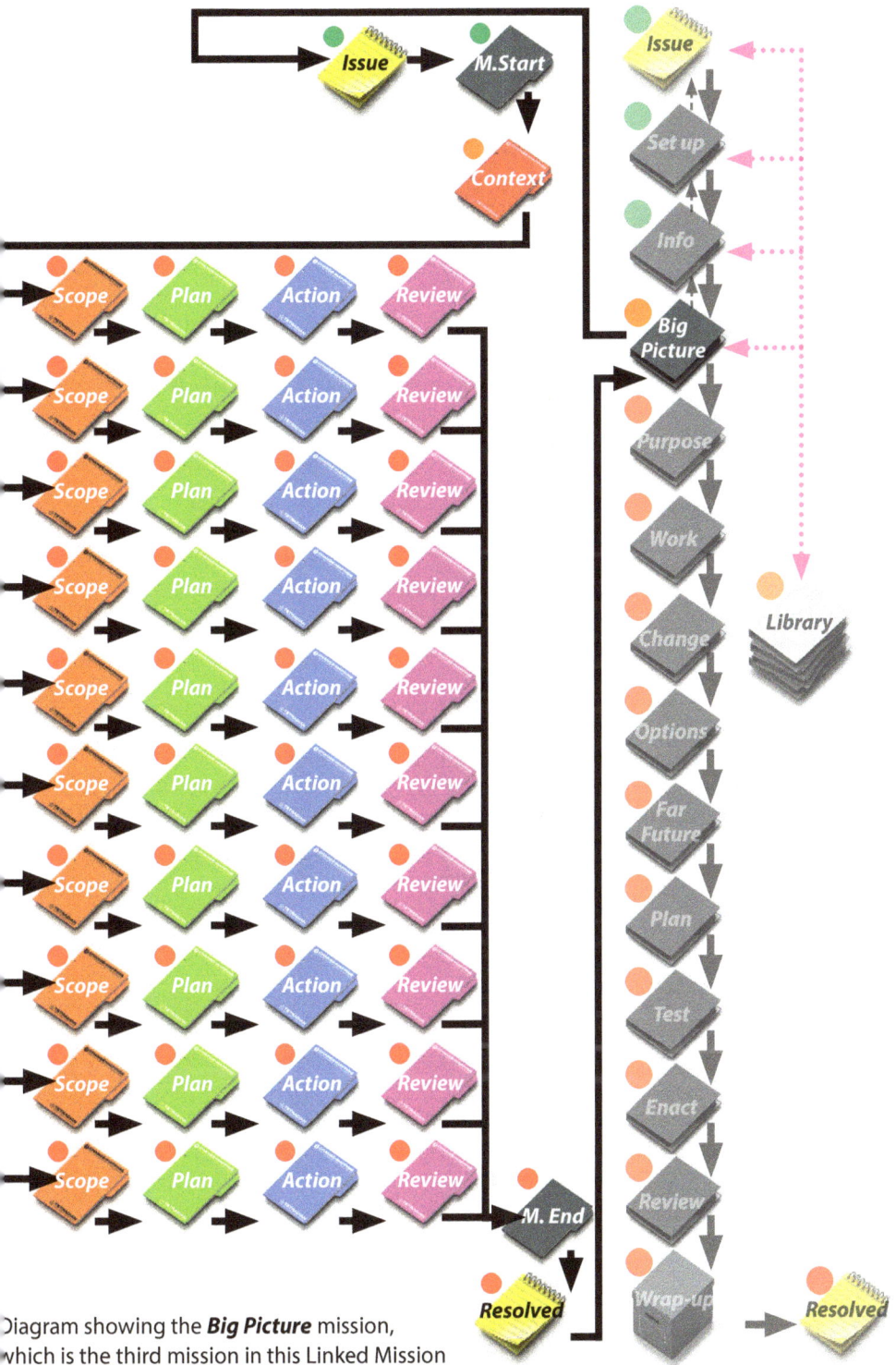

Diagram showing the **Big Picture** mission,
which is the third mission in this Linked Mission

Using non-Change-mapping tools in this mission

- Root cause analysis
- Quality management
- H & S management
- PEST tool
- BCG Matrix

These tools could be used alongside the questions shown on the right, to help define where the issue fits into the overall enterprise.

An important note

The tool shown on the right has two sections.
The top section typically will be filled during a separate Linked Mission which explores the enterprise. The lower dashed section is enterprise information which you fill in within your Linked Mission.

How to use this mission

What is the mission used for?

This mission is used to provide an overview of the enterprise and to see how the issue raised relates to the enterprise.
This will act as a check that resolving the issue will support the enterprise, which will be referenced throughout the Linked Mission.

What needs to be done before using this mission tool?

This mission is set-up using standard *Change-mapping (Book 1, page 18)*. As the main focus of this mission will be exploring or resolving the issue, a large amount of the enterprise information would take time to assemble. It is recommended to have the Main Library supply enterprise information to the people running this mission *(see page 64)*.

Who is typically involved in this mission?

Strategy teams, Business transformation experts, and Business architects.

Warning signs while running the mission

- Rushing through this mission and ignoring the context that your issue is part of.
- Losing focus while exploring the context which can lead to wasted time.
- Conversely staying too rigidly to a biased view of the context with pre-conceived ideas.

What works well with this mission?

- Γ The *Sense-making tool* can be useful when exploring the context of an issue *(Book 2, page 10)*.
- Θ The *Holomap tool* *(Book 2, page 22)* to explore stakeholders within the enterprise.
- ☰ The *Value tool* *(Book 2, page 6)* to set explore what is valued within the enterprise.
- Σ The *Visioning tool* *(Book 2, page 14)* to explore what are the stakeholders vision for the enterprise.
- Φ The *Basic Context tool 2/3/4* tools *(Book 1, page 72)* to explore the enterprise and its relationship to your issue.

Mission 3 of 13 *Answer all questions using Change-mapping techniques (Book1, page 18).*

What is the enterprise trying to address? Γ
Australia's construction industry generates billions of dollars in revenue, helping to build infrastructure, business assets and homes across the country.

What are the key factors which affect the enterprise? Γ
Sustainability, Arbitration, Structured negotiations, Financial issues Tenders, Building and other permits, Contract law, Extensions of time Drafting construction contracts and others (source, wikipedia)

Who are the key stakeholders in the enterprise? Θ
Developers, suppliers, clients, work-force, legal teams (our area), Government, People who are not involved may be affected by the developments.

What is valued within the enterprise? Ξ
Trust is one of the key values within the enterprise. For our involvement this would mean if a legal document and legal counsel are promised at 9.00 am Monday in Brisbane, they need to be there at the specified time.

What is the stakeholder's vision for the enterprise? Σ
Having a clear up-to-date picture of the state of the construction industry. Being aware and able to react to forces which can influence the sector, before it becomes too difficult and costly.

What factors affect the overall enterprise?
Politics affect the enterprise greatly, such as changes in policy. Economics, the construction sector has increased revenue by 2% in the last year. Social, an increased demand for sustainability. Technology, cloud based computers and storage are game changers.

What are the laws, standards and regulations for the enterprise? Φ
We have a within the Library information about the laws, standards and regulations within the enterprise. For example, Australian construction law.

What are the success criteria for the enterprise? Φ
People will have usable information which can inform decision-making.

How does the issue raised relate to the overall enterprise? Γ
We provide legal counsel to key stakeholders, we use ERP software to move our assets and staff at the right time and location. As we are opening an office in London our ERP is struggling with the increased demands.

How does the issue raised support the enterprise? Γ
The updated ERP software would allow us to provide a more up-to date picture of what our stakeholders require and then meet those needs.

The *Purpose* mission
Clarifying your organisation's purpose

In brief
In this part of the Linked Mission we explore how we will clarify if exploring and ultimately resolving the issue aligns with our organisation's purpose. For example, if we imagine a city council want to make the city more sustainable, why is this important to the city council?

Who are we and why do we do what we do?

At first it might seem that your organisation's purpose is to make money and that resolving your issue will make you more money. But if you remove money, why does your organisation do what it does? Usually it is to make things better for all within the enterprise. Doing good usually gives people a sense of purpose and pride. Various quotes echo this view and if resolving your issue doesn't align with your purpose, why do it? This mission is used to cross-check that your organisation's values align with the issue you want to resolve.

Worked example

Continuing our example, the strategy team want to update the ERP, but they have also been asked to cross-check that resolving the issue aligns with the legal firm's purpose. "Our purpose is just to make money isn't it?" says one of the team. But when they start to think about it, there are easier ways to make money, yet they do what they do.

Helping people navigate the law is what gives them purpose and pride in what they do. They again ask the main Library for information to help cross-check updating ERP with the organisation and their purpose. A quick check shows that ERP would strongly support their purpose.

They also found information that would help others in the legal firm and so sent it to the main Library for their reference. They also cross-checked with the previous mission to see that everything all lined up.

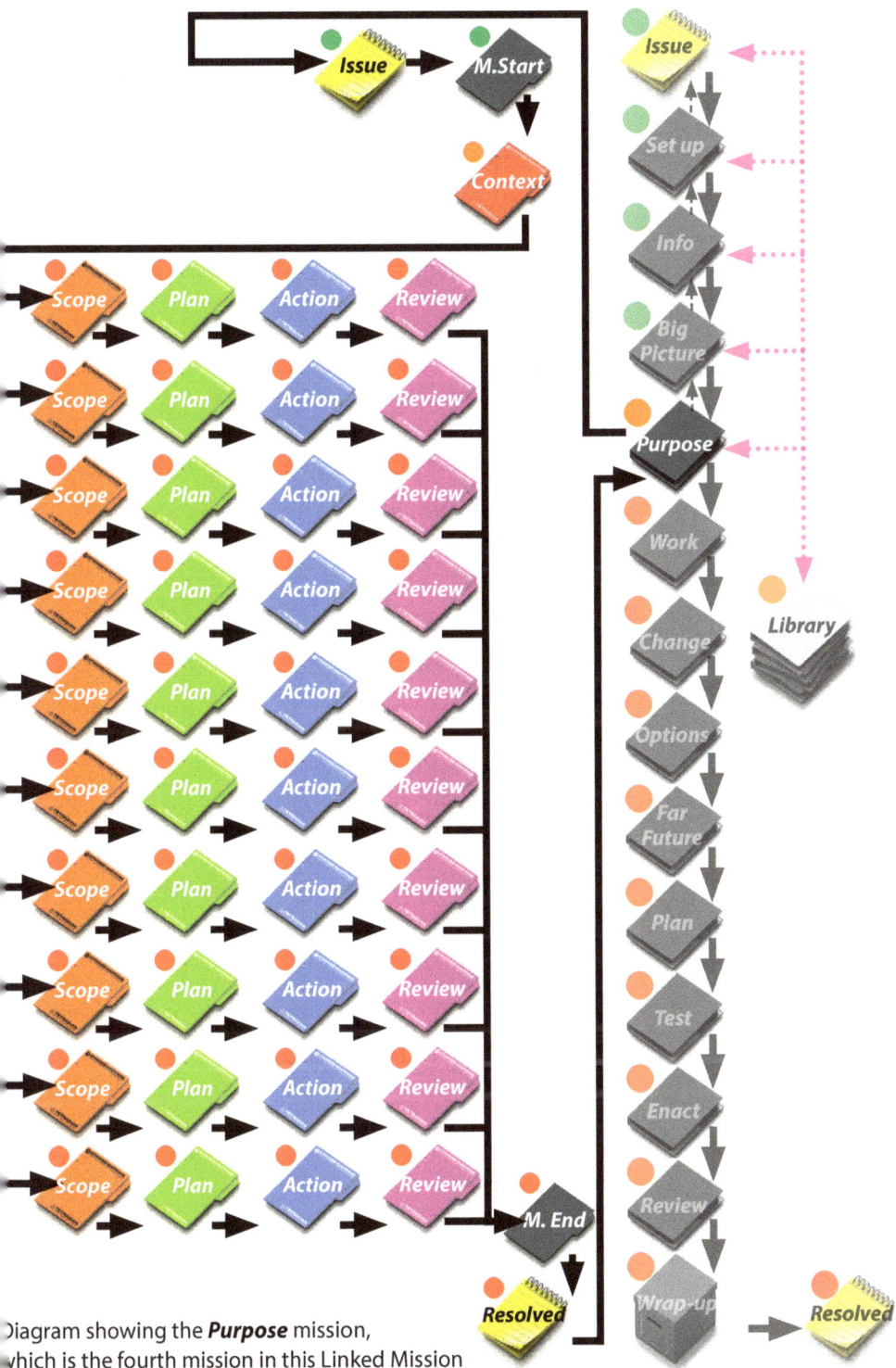

Diagram showing the **Purpose** mission,
which is the fourth mission in this Linked Mission

Using non-Change-mapping tools in this mission

• *Business case*
• *Risk management**
• *Ansoff Matrix*
These tools could be used alongside the questions shown on the right, to help define where the issue fits into your organisation's purpose.
*Risk can also offer new opportunities (See Book 2, page 74, where Risk is part of the SCORE tool).

How to use this mission
What is the mission used for?

This mission is used to provide an overview of the organisation's purpose and to see how the issue raised relate to their purpose. This will act as a checklist that resolving the issue will support the purpose, which will be referenced throughout the Linked Mission.

What needs to be done before using this mission tool?

This mission is set-up using standard *Change-mapping (Book 1, page 18).* As the main focus of this mission will be exploring or resolving the issue, a large amount of the purpose information would take time to assemble. It is recommended to have the Main Library supply purpose information to the people running this mission *(see page 64).*

Who is typically involved in this mission?

Strategy teams, Business transformation experts, and Business architects.

Warning signs while running the mission

• Allowing your organisation's purpose to take priority over the enterprise. Ideally they should be in balance.
• The purpose to be a meaningless statement which is impossible to actually enact.
• The purpose is pushed to one side in the quest to resolve the issue.

What works well with this mission?

Γ The **SEMPER tool** *(Book 2, page 60)* to can be used to provide evidence that your purpose is being enacted as you hope it is. This would likely involve a Nested-Mission *(Book 1, page 114)* to gather evidence that staff agree that the organisation's purpose is easy to enact.

Δ The **Effectiveness tool** *(Book 2, page 34)* to provide criteria for success in the mission.

Θ The **Basic Context tools 2,3,4** *(Book 1, page 72)* to provide criteria for success in the mission.

☰ Refer to your notes in the **Big Picture** mission *(Page 16)* to cross-check that the enterprise and your purpose align.

Purpose mission tool

Mission identification: Linked Mission to update our Legal firm's ERP system
2OCTOBER2032-MISSION-02048

Mission 4 of 13 *Answer all questions using Change-mapping techniques (Book1, page 18).*

What is the purpose of your organisation?
We strive to help all of those involved in construction navigate the law.
So that they can build elegant, safe and sustainable buildings which
improve our country.

Where in the enterprise does the organisation position itself?
Our founders helped a Sydney based construction company in 1903
draft contract law to protect their company. Our founders wanted to help
those in the construction industry as they had family in that sector.

How does the enterprise shape your purpose?
The construction industry of which we are part, is the reason we exist.
If the enterprise changed and didn't value workers rights for example, we
would want to change our involvement.

How does your purpose consider social and global concerns?
Sustainability in building construction, additionally we use sustainable
practices. We used the SEMPER tool (Book 2, page 60) to seek evidence that
staff agree that our purpose inspires and does consider social and global

How does your purpose inspire personal commitment by staff members?
We have a sustainability initiative and staff development schemes.
We used the SEMPER tool to seek evidence that staff agree that our purpose
inspires commitment.

How is your purpose simple and easy to apply in practice?
Our website gives a clear definition of our purpose as well we have training
days. We used the SEMPER tool to seek evidence that staff agree that our
purpose is easy to apply in practice.

How does your purpose provide clear guidelines to manage change?
This is an area we are working on. (INSIGHT A mission to explore this).
We used the SEMPER tool to seek evidence that staff agree that our purpose
provides clear guidelines to manage change .

How does your purpose support and align with the enterprise?
We also cross-checked with the last mission. We used the SEMPER tool to
seek evidence that staff agree that our purpose aligns with the enterprise.

How will resolving your issue demonstrate your organisation's purpose?
Being able to effectively meet our clients needs but not at the expense of our
staff, will stay true to our purpose.

How does the issue raised support your organisation's purpose?
Resolving the issue we feel stays true to our organisation's purpose.
Updating the ERP would improve our offer and help us assist our clients
as effectively as possible.

The *Work* mission
Understanding how your organisation functions

In brief

In this part of the Linked Mission we explore how our organisation functions and in part if we have the capabilities to resolve the issue raised. For example, how does the city council function presently, do they have the skills to make their city more sustainable?

How do we do what we do?

When an issue is raised, it often assumes that a change is required. Before changing something it makes sense to fully understand *what* you are changing.

This mission is used to set a bench-mark of what *is*, before enacting change. This will give something to gauge if the changes actually change anything and more importantly change the right things. Part of this information will be gathered from the Library to save time and avoid bias.

In addition this mission will be used to gather information about the organisation which can be of use for others.

Worked example

In our example the strategy team needed to find out if updating ERP would improve how their legal firm functioned But they first needed to see how it functioned, for all they knew ERP might not even impact on how the firm operated. They consulted the main Library for information about how the organisation functioned, to see if ERP or what it does was mentioned. They also interviewed stakeholders to see what they felt impacted on how they work. This gave the strategy team a good representation of how the legal firm operated currently. This base of information would be vital for measuring what the stakeholders feel needed to change and if updating the ERP would help the stakeholders.

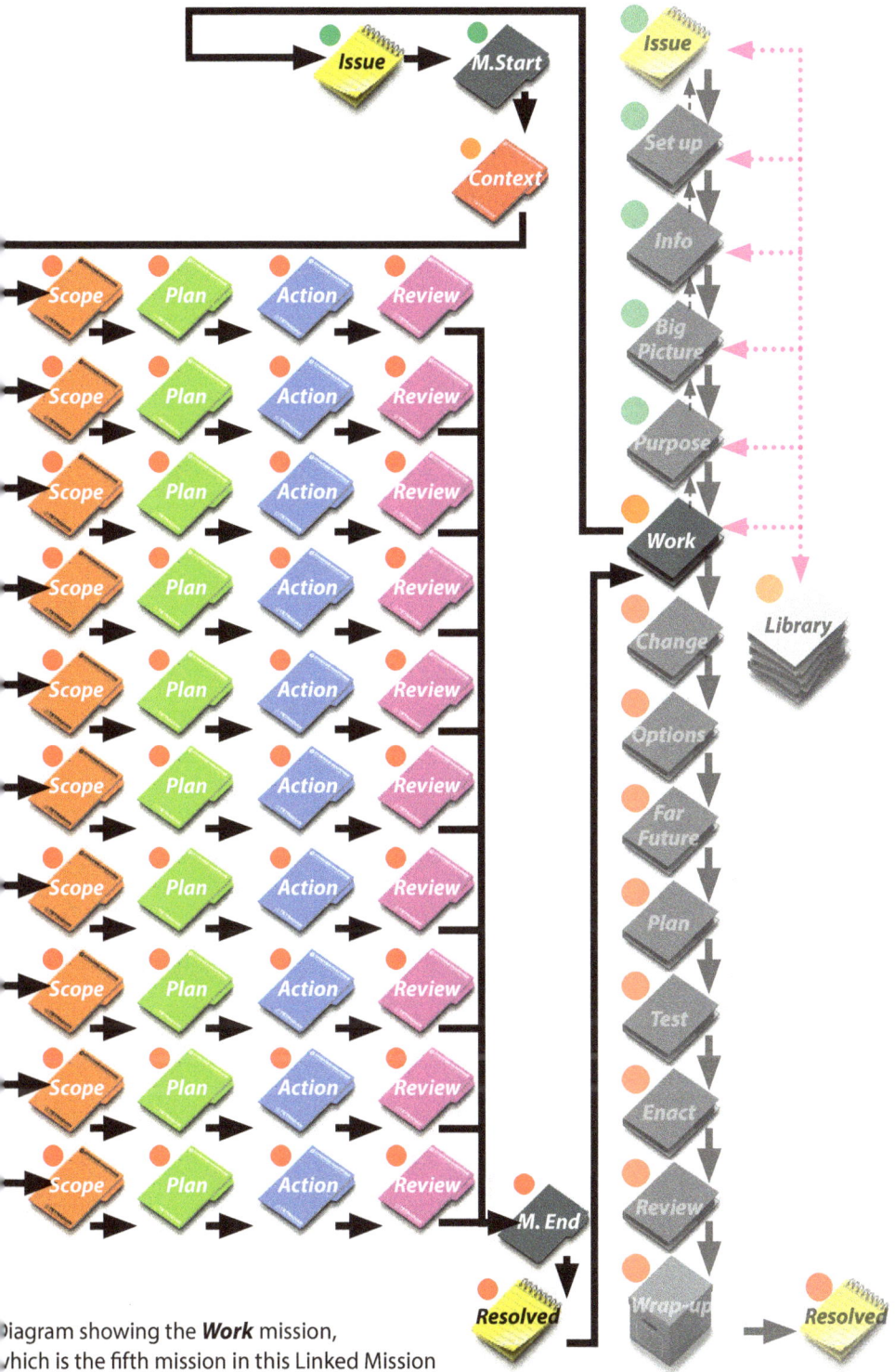

Diagram showing the **Work** mission,
which is the fifth mission in this Linked Mission

Using non-Change-mapping tools in this mission

Business case
Porter's value chain
Risk management*
Four Ps
Business Model Canvas
These tools could be used alongside the questions shown on the right, to help define where the issue fits into how your organisation functions. *Risk can also offer new opportunities (See Book 2, page 74, where Risk is part of the SCORE tool).

How to use this mission

What is the mission used for?

This mission is used to provide an overview of how the organisation functions and to see how the issue raised relates to their effectiveness. What is found within this mission will act as evidence, that resolving the issue will support that effectiveness, which will then be referenced throughout the entire Linked Mission.

What needs to be done before using this mission tool?

This mission is set-up using standard *Change-mapping (Book 1, page 18)*. As the main focus of this mission will be exploring or resolving the issue, a large amount of the effectiveness information would take time to assemble. It is recommended to have the Main Library supply effectiveness information to the people running this mission *(see page 64)*.

Who is typically involved in this mission?

Strategy teams, Business transformation experts, and Business architects.

Warning signs while running the mission

- Making the facts fit your theory *(for example telling people they need better computers, when actually they may need better training)*.
- Influencing those you observe, so that they don't function as they typically would.

What works well with this mission?

Γ Check the Big Picture/Purpose missions for your results. See pages 16 and 20.

Δ The **SEMPER tool** *(Book 2, page 60)* to establish if staff members feel they can function effectively.

Θ The **Inside/Out tool** *(Book 2, page 40)* to evaluate the roles and tasks within your organisation.

Λ The **Notes tool** *(Book 2, page 64)* to evaluate who does what within your organisation.

Ξ The **Value tool** *(Book 2, page 6)* to explore what is valued within your organisation.

Φ The **Effectiveness tool** *(Book 2, page 34)* to describe your organisation's effectiveness standards.

Ψ The **SCORE tool** *(Book 2, page 74)* to map your organisation's capabilities to resolve an issue.

Ω The **Enterprise Canvas tool** *(Book 2, page 18)* to describe how your organisation interacts with stakeholders.

Mission 5 of 13 *Answer all questions using Change-mapping techniques (Book1, page 18).*

What are the key factors which affect your organisation?
New government legislation has greatly affected how we and our clients
do business

Γ Φ Θ

Who are the key stakeholders inside your organisation?
We used the NOTES tool (Book2, page 64) to provide a picture of our
stakeholders internally. For example our IT team, lawyers and the strategy
teams are some of our key internal stakeholders.

Γ Ω Λ

What is valued within the organisation?
Trust. Confidentiality. Accuracy are three paramount values.
(INSIGHT does the new ERP system support these values,
for example Cloud security?)

Ξ Δ

Who does what and how within your organisation?
This of course is a huge question. We used various tools (see page left) to
map out all the people and what they do. For example our lawyers travel to
meetings to advise clients.

Ω Λ Θ

What physical, virtual, relational and aspirational assets does the org. use?
One example would be legal documents. These are often THE only way that
information can be shared. The ERP system has to make sure these are in the
right place at the right time.

Ω Λ Θ

What are the barriers that impede you completing tasks?
A recent barrier has been a call from staff to be able to work from home.
ERP has helped make this happen. Updated ERP would increase
this flexibility.

Ψ

How does the issue raised, relate to the overall organisation?
Managing the times and locations of assets and people is critical to how our
legal firm operates. Updated ERP should (if it works) improve
this management.

Γ

How does the issue raised, improve your organisation's effectiveness?
ERP allows us to have a real time picture of where assets are and when they
will arrive. As well making sure our skilled lawyers are not wasting time sat
in airports rather than in the clients offices.

Φ

Does your organisation have the capabilities to resolve the issue?
We have an experienced IT team who have handled a large scale update a few years
ago. We will use the SCORE tool (See tools left) to evaluate our capabilities to resolve
the issue, if it is found that resolving the issue supports below.)

Ψ

Does resolving the issue support your organisation, purpose and the enterprise?
We feel that updating the ERP will support all stakeholders, if there was a
discrepancy then we would question if resolving the issue was justified.

Γ

The *Change* mission
Establishing what needs to change

In brief

In this part of the Linked Mission we explore what we want to change, not how we bring about that change. For example, does the city want to be more sustainable in one particular area? In our example, they want more green spaces to improve air quality and make the city a more pleasant place to live.

What do we want to change?

This mission is not concerned with *how* to change things, rather *what* things need to change.

This involves asking stakeholders what *they* feel needs to change, rather than assuming what they need.

This is done in two parts, with the first being to ask what they feel needs to change without mentioning the issue to be resolved, to avoid bias. The second part involves enquiring if they feel that resolving the issue will improve how they function inside the organisation.

Worked example

In our example the strategy team wanted to find out what the lawyers, clients and other stakeholders felt needed to change. Some of their ideas were seen as too costly for this time, while others were more practical. The team also referenced the earlier missions to see if what people wanted to change aligned with was found earlier, such as the Big Picture.

After this unbiased enquiry the team asked if stakeholders felt that resolving the issue would improve effectiveness. Typically ERP would be used to help in various tasks such as making sure that legal documents were sent to the right office at the right time. Updating the ERP would help make this kind of task easier. But if no-one felt that updating the ERP would benefit them, then this would call into doubt if they should update the ERP.

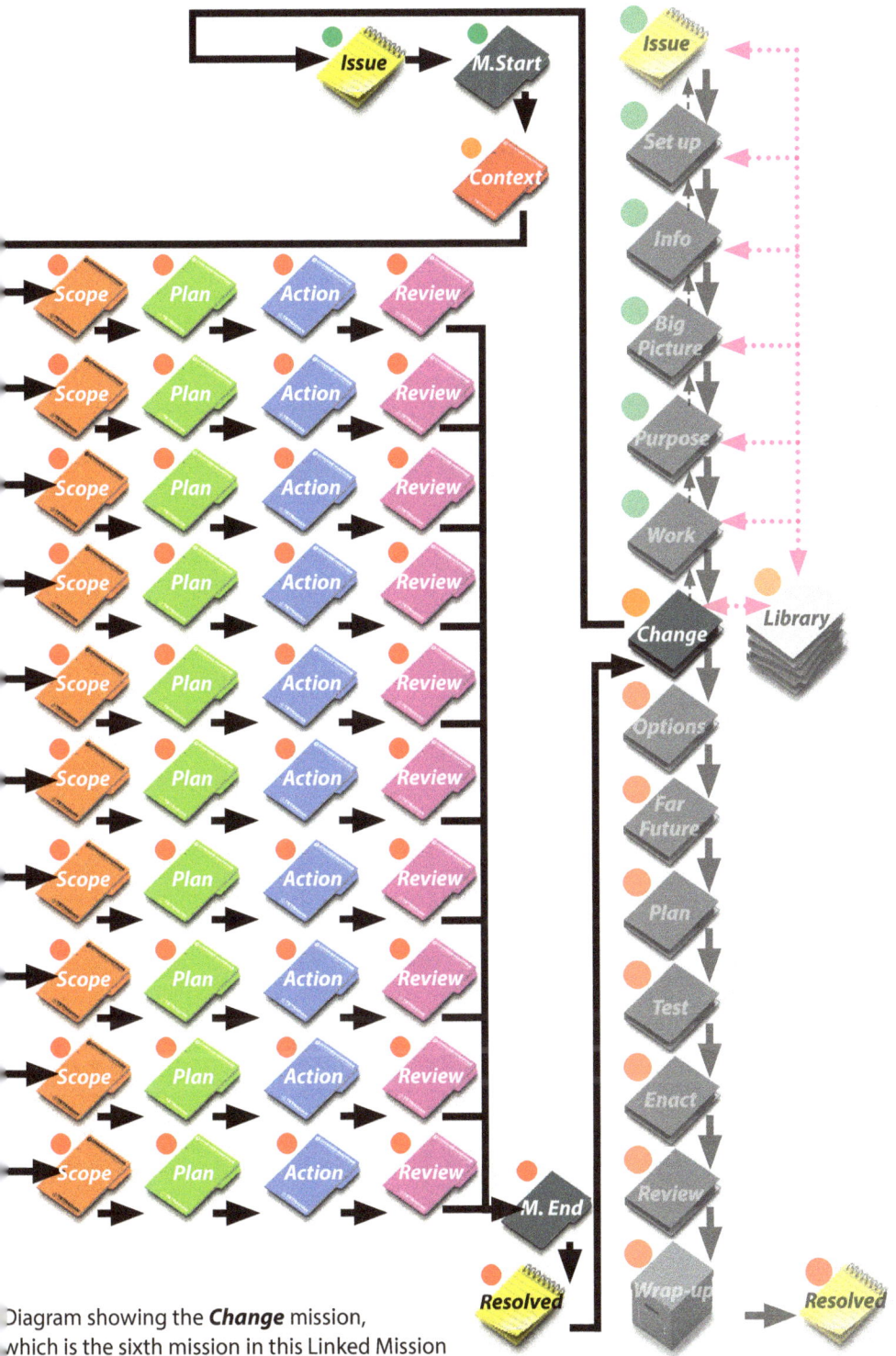

Diagram showing the **Change** mission,
which is the sixth mission in this Linked Mission

Using non-Change-mapping tools in this mission

Using non-Change-mapping tools in this mission

- *Change management*
- *John Kotter's 8-Step Process for Leading Change*
- *Role Playing*
- *MoSCoW tool*
- *Business Capability tools*
- *Trade-offs tools*
- *Service/Product Specification documents*

These tools could be used alongside the questions shown on the right, to help define if change is required and what needs to change.

An important note

The top section of the tool asks what stakeholders feel needs to change. If the issue raised is not mentioned, this could suggest it might not be worth solving.

The dashed line box acts as a gateway. Here you decide if you want to resolve your issue based on what was found in earlier missions.

How to use this mission

What is the mission used for?

This mission is used to provide an overview of what stakeholders believe needs to change, even if that shows that resolving the issue won't bring about the desired outcome. It is also used to decide if you want to resolve your issue or leave things unchanged.

What needs to be done before using this mission tool?

This mission is set-up using standard *Change-mapping (Book page 18)*. Remember to reference the earlier missions to make sure the proposed changes stay true to the enterprise, etc.

Who is typically involved in this mission?

Business analysts, Business change analysts, Process teams and Governance teams *(the previous missions should have identified who these are)*.
Stakeholders who will be affected by the issue being resolved

Warning signs while running the mission

- Making the facts fit your theory
- Influencing those you interview, so that they don't function as they typically would.
- Having experts tell the people who do the work, how to do their work better with little or no respect.
- Ignoring external factors to your organisation's functioning, such as when you are not the start or end of a process.

What works well with this mission?

Γ Cross check what was found in the earlier missions to establish what is now and why it *might* need changing, and that any change stays true to the vision and values of the enterprise.

Δ The **Guide tool** *(Book 2, page 26)* to define what can change and what can not within your organisation.

Σ The **Knock-on effects tool** *(Book 2, page 68)* to explore the possible consequences of resolving your issue.

Φ The **Decision tool** *(Book 2, page 44)* to establish how decisions such as change are made inside your organisation.

Mission identification: Linked Mission to update our Legal firm's ERP system.
20CTOBER2032-MISSION-02048

Mission 6 of 13 *Answer all questions using Change-mapping techniques (Book1, page 18).*

What needs to change within the organisation *(Physical)*? **Γ**
Having hardware which will allow us to work remotely. Having legal documents transported safely and promptly. We rely on ERP to make sure we can function effectively across the country.

What needs to change within the organisation *(Virtual)*? **Γ** **Λ**
Better sharing of real time information, wherever we are . For example if a clients meeting has been moved forward by a few hours we can re-route an important document.

What needs to change within the organisation *(Relational)*? **Γ**
The relationships with clients and suppliers are vital. Our staff need a healthy work-life balance. They mentioned how enterprise resource management and ERP software could help maintain happy motivated staff members.

What needs to change within the organisation *(Aspirational)*? **Γ**
We don't feel that our aspirations need to change, if they were to then our organisation would change. (SEE THE PURPOSE MISSION, page 20)

What can change and what can't within the organisation? **Γ** **Δ**
Accuracy and confidentiality and trust has to be maintained. For example any computer system has to adhere to those values

How will the issue raised bring effective change? **Γ** **Σ**
With more staff working from home for extended periods, cloud based ERP (part of the new update) will improve working conditions.

What are the barriers to instigate the proposed change? **Γ** **Σ**
Staff are used to the current system, so we need to communicate the benefits of updating the ERP software and that the change will not affect their ability to do their work.

What are the unexpected consequences of the proposed change? **Λ** **Σ**
As the new update is cloud based, security could be a factor. As most of our work is highly confidential, security is paramount.

How do you feel that you should resolve the issue, based on our research? **Γ** **Φ**
Based on what we have found in the missions, including this one, we feel that resolving the issue will bring beneficial change. How we will initiate that change will be explored in the following mission.

What needs to change? When, Where, Who? Available initial budget? **Φ**
To bring about the desired change we will update the ERP software in all our offices within 18 months for a proposed budget of AU$ 6,000,000.

Download a blank copy at: www.changemappingbook.com/advanced-change-mapping-book

The *Options* mission
Exploring options to bring about change

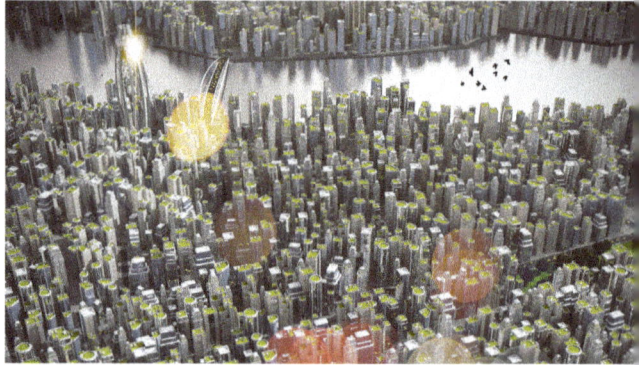

In brief
In this part of the Linked Mission we explore what are our options to bring about our desired change. For example, our city wants to have more green spaces. What options do they have to make this happen? In our simple example they choose an option to make more skyscrapers have roof top gardens. Helping biodiversity, improving air quality and improving citizen's lives.

What are our options to enact change?

The previous missions were used to confirm that the issue raised did warrant being resolved. This mission is used to explore options to effectively bring about change.

The mission looks at various options, rather than just what is done before. Often people asked *"Why do you do it that way?"* answer *"We have always done it that way"*. There may be better ways of resolving the issue. Part of this mission involves asking experts and stakeholders how to resolve the issue instead of unquestioningly using tried and tested methods.

Worked example

The strategy team consulted with the IT team, as they had implemented the last ERP solution. Both teams discussed what options they had for the new ERP update. Most wanted to stick with their current vendor as they knew how it all worked. The current solution didn't seem set up for international clients. They used part of the mission to explore other vendors and found a different ERP provider which seemed to offer much more than their current one.

They decided to trial the new vendor cautiously before a full roll-out. They realised if they had jumped straight to the Plan Mission (see right) then they would have ended up planning for the wrong solution to their issue.

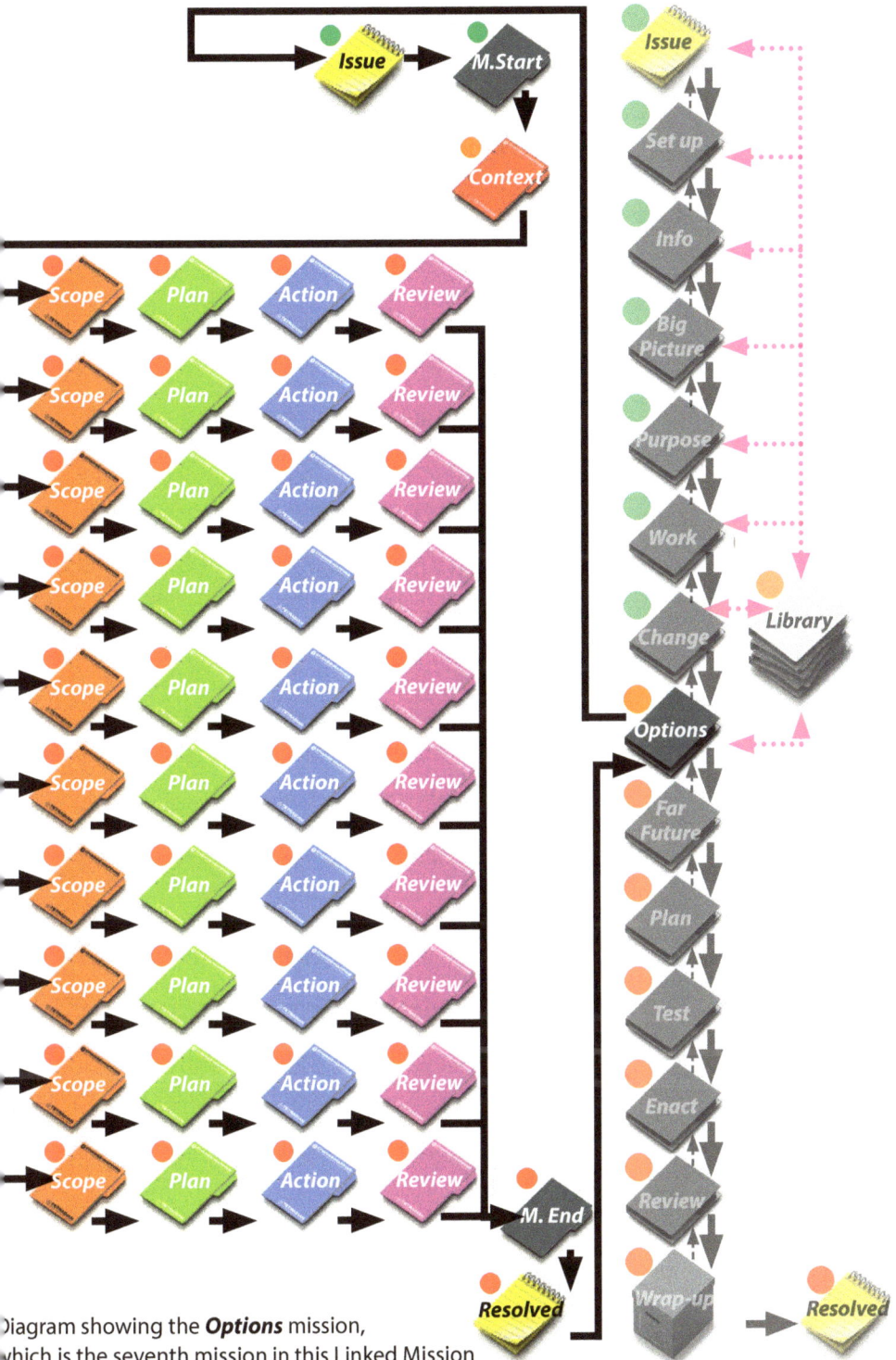

Diagram showing the **Options** mission,
which is the seventh mission in this Linked Mission

*Using non-Change-mapping
tools in this mission*
• *Work Breakdown structure*
• *MoSCoW tool*
• *RACI tool*
• *Disaster recovery plan*
*These tools could be used
alongside the questions shown
on the right, to help identify if
change is required and what
needs to change.*

How to use this mission
How can this mission help you?
This mission is used to explore options to bring about the
desired change.

What needs to be done before using this mission tool?
This mission is set-up using standard *Change-mapping (Book
1, page 18)*. Remember to reference the earlier missions to
make sure the proposed changes stay true to the enterprise,
organisation's purpose and more.

Who is typically involved in this mission?
Process designers, System designers, Tech leads, Process lead
Stakeholders with responsibility such as for safety, quality,
security and so on. Stakeholders who will be affected by the
issue being resolved.

Warning signs while running the mission
• Choosing the first option without exploring other options.
• Not allowing for true innovation, there may be a truly
  innovative unorthodox solution.
• Ridiculing those that offer different solutions.
• Having a room full of experts, who say we always do it that
  way, without knowing why they do it that way.
• Conversely allowing the mission to waste time with
  wild ideas.
• Submitting to analysis-paralysis *(Book 1, page 54)*.
• Jumping to the plan, without considering future implication

---

What works well with this mission?
Γ Cross check what was found in the earlier missions to
establish what the situation is now and why it *might* need
changing, and that any change stays true to the vision and
values of the enterprise.
Δ The **Leadership tool** *(Book 2, page 48)* to explore creating a
disaster recovery plan.
Θ The **Knock-on effects tool** *(Book 2, page 68)* to explore the
possible consequences of resolving your issue.
Λ The **SCORE tool** *(Book 2, page 74)* to explore the options your
organisation has, to resolve your issue and the risks involved.
Ξ The **Where to start tool** *(Book 2, page 78)* to explore how your
organisation can resolve your issue.

Options mission tool

CHANGE→MAPPING
CONNECTING BUSINESS TOOLS TO MANAGE CHANGE

Mission identification: Linked Mission to update our Legal firm's ERP system
20CTOBER2032-MISSION-02048

Mission 7 of 13 *Answer all questions using Change-mapping techniques (Book1, page 18).*

What are the key areas that need to be solved?
A cloud based ERP solution which is fully secure and can be customised in the future if required. We need to be able to update the ERP without causing mayhem to our legal firm's staff members and clients.

What are our options to bring about the desired change?
We can stick with our current ERP vendor or we could use a new vendor. We could have a custom ERP solution designed for us, which would be very expensive.

What is a mild option and what is a wild option to bring change?
Most probably the mildest option would involve staying with our current vendor, who we know. But there are certain services they don't offer, which we are starting to need which is why a wilder option might be better such as a new vendor.

Is our chosen option: technology led or user led?
A mixture, at the moment we are fitting around the ERP software, but it would be better if it fitted around us. We should ask users of the ERP software what they need and what the update is proposing to change.

If the solution failed, how would we do disaster recovery?
In the Testing mission we will need to test the ERP update in difficult conditions to inform the creation of a relevant disaster recovery plan. But more than anything, this needs investigating BEFORE the actual update!

If one part of the solution failed, how would it affect the rest of the solution?
Again the Testing mission should inform us about this. We need to investigate key areas that impact other areas. Bottlenecks that could be worked around. For example a bridge that all key roads go through, rather than a side road.

What are the potential benefits of your proposed option?
This update would allow us to react to client requirements much quicker and more effectively. It may also allow us to cater for airport construction requirements, which has been too specialised for us in the past.

Who will produce a final resolution, and what skills they will need?
Our new vendor will create the new ERP software. Our IT team will perform the update. INSIGHT> The IT team need to be fully up to speed with the new ERP software, otherwise if the situation changed drastically, they could struggle.

What are the potential consequences of your chosen option?
Increase in mistakes, complaints from users, clients and other stakeholders. This could escalate and cause clients to leave if it became severe.

Which option do you want to choose?
We will trial a new vendor who will provide updated ERP, as this allows a more customised approach, but with proper testing. Hope for the best, plan for the worst...

Download a blank copy at: *www.changemappingbook.com/advanced-change-mapping-book*

The *Far Future* mission
What happens after the issue is resolved?

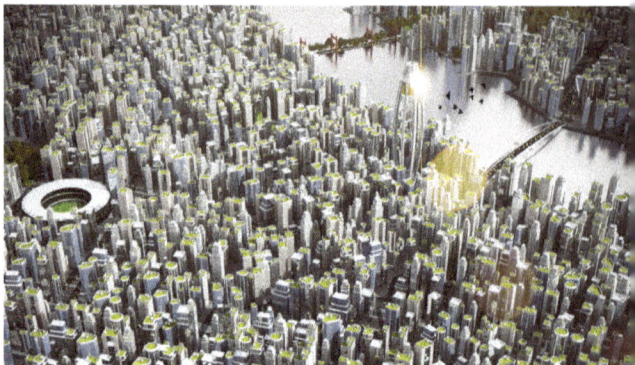

In brief

In this part of the Linked Mission we explore what happens after our issue is resolved. In our city example, how might the skyscraper roof top gardens be decommissioned, if required? What are the unforeseen consequences of having roof top gardens? What are the unexpected benefits as well?

What happens after we have succeeded?

In the quest to resolve an issue, worrying about what happens *after* you have resolved the issue might not seem that important. But are you solving a small problem now and creating an even bigger problem in the future?

This mission is used to explore how your chosen option to resolve an issue might cause other issues in the future.

In addition the mission looks at how other people might have to disassemble your solution.

Worked example

Our legal firm is planning to update their ERP software from version 1 to version 2. All of the team are planning how the ERP software update will actually be implemented.

Until one of them asks "What happens when V2 needs updating?". Of course one day, even this update will need to be replaced or even decommissioned. Although this might not happen for some years, what they choose to do now may force their hand in the future.

Also how would the person a few years in the future know what people did and why? The IT team felt that they should leave a record of what was done and why, so that in the future time wouldn't be wasted retracing people's steps.

They also wanted to check that their ERP vendor was a stable company and what to do if they went out of business or the vendor was taken over.

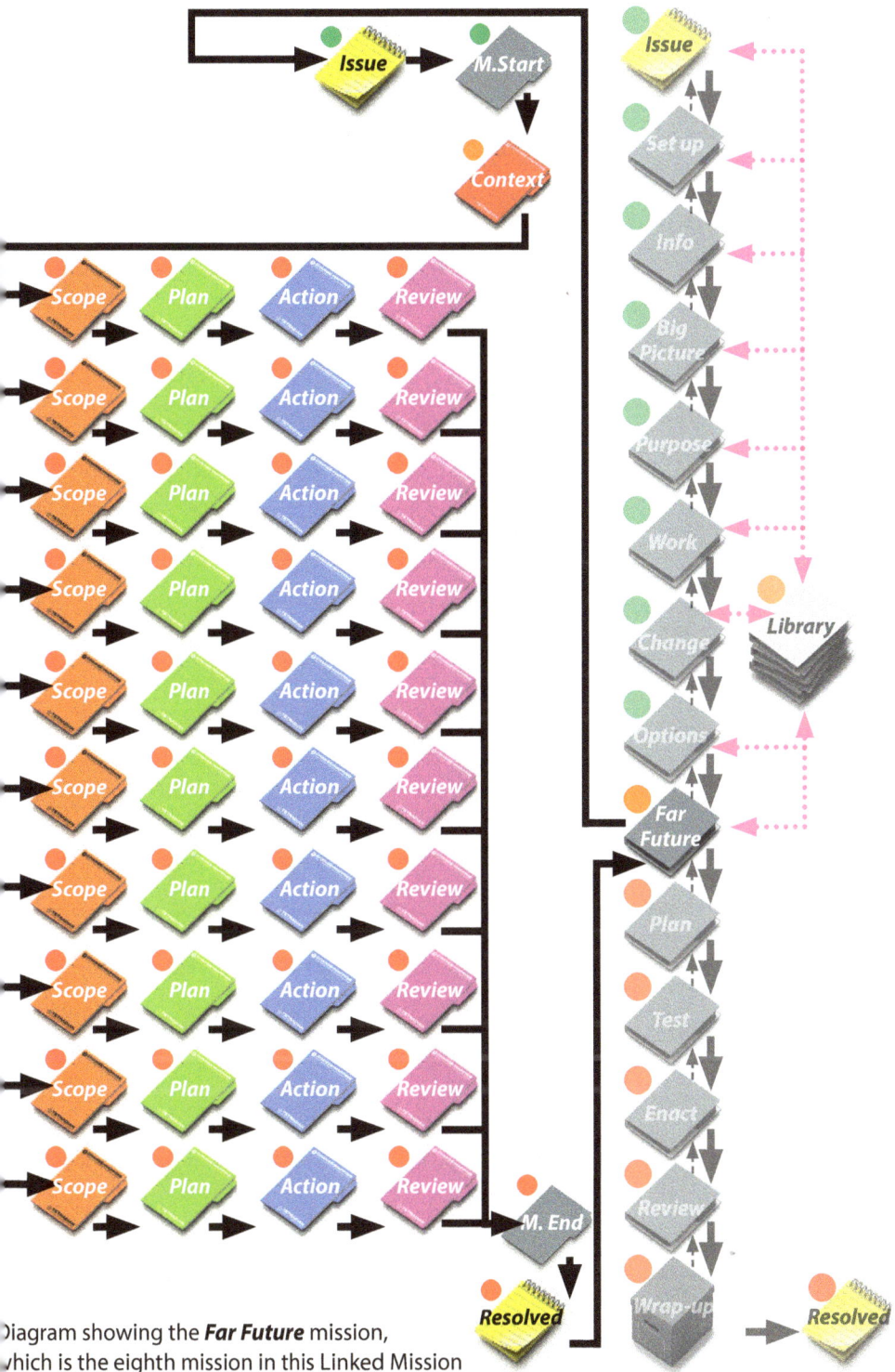

Diagram showing the **Far Future** mission,
which is the eighth mission in this Linked Mission

Using non-Change-mapping tools in this mission

- Design for disassembly
- Software decommissioning
- Tools for Futures Thinking and Foresight across UK Government
- Business continuity plan
- Disaster recovery plan
- Transition plan
- Tools which examine what happens after an issue is resolved
- Trade-offs tools
- Far future tools

These web-searches could be used alongside the questions shown on the right, to explore how you can plan for the far future.

How to use this mission

What is the mission used for?

This mission is used to consider how somebody in the future may have to take apart your solution, and if this will influence the design of your solution.

What needs to be done before using this mission tool?

This mission is set up using standard *Change-mapping (Book page 18)*. Most likely you will be jumping between *missions 6-10* refining your plan, so what is found here may shape your solution to your issue.

Who is typically involved in this type of mission?

Risk management, Innovation teams, Futures teams and Strategy teams.

Warning signs while running the mission

- Planning to resolve an issue with no consideration about how the resolution will itself be DDR *(see right)*.
- Having no records of how your solution was constructed, so that somebody in the future would be unable to deconstruct your solution, if required.
- Having no plans for how you might transition from a current solution to a newer solution, such as transitioning from having an airport with two terminals to three terminals.

What works well with this mission?

- The **Knock-on effects tool** *(Book 2, page 68)* to explore the unexpected consequences of resolving issues.
- The **SCAN tool** *(Book 2, page 82)* to explore the uncertainties when resolving an issue.
- The **Holomap tool** *(Book 2, page 22)* to explore possible future stakeholders within the enterprise.
- The **Sense-making tool** *(Book 2, page 10)* to explore future potential issues.
- The **Where to start tool** *(Book 2, page 78)* to explore how to resolve an unknown issue.

Mission identification: Linked Mission to update our Legal firm's ERP system.
20CTOBER2032-MISSION-02048

Mission 8 of 13 *Answer all questions using Change-mapping techniques (Book 1, page 18).*

How long is the solution to your issue intended to last?
We imagine that the updated ERP will have a lifetime of six years before
it will need to updated again.

What happens after that time (see above)?
Most likely we will need to go through a similar process, to maintain
business continuity.

How will your solution be Decommissioned, Disassembled or Replaced (DDR)?
Unless there is a major shift in technology and how we work we would replace
the updated ERP with a new update. So currently we are using ERP V1, we
want to update to ERP V2 and in six years ERP V3 (if it exists!). If updates
are continued?

Θ
X

Who, what, what budget, when, where, how would the DDR be done?
We would need to start to explore this before six years, but we assume a
similar price as the V2 update, not taking account of inflation. Cost of
labour increases, material costs increase and so on.

X

What issues might arise trying to complete DDR?
We could become to dependent on our current vendor, that if they stopped
trading we could find it much harder to migrate to a new provider.

Θ
Φ

How would you DDR a resolved issue?
If we had to decommission the new update in a few years it would be a major
undertaking. Disassembling would result from major shift in business focus.
Replacing our updated ERP in a few years... (NESTED MISSION, to find out?).

X

What kind of records would you keep to assist with DDR in the future?
When we do the current update (V1 to V2) we need detailed notes that showed
what we did, so that people in the future can follow the path of what we did
and why. (INSIGHT, we need to plan for this before the ENACT mission).

X
Σ

How would you transition from the old to the new?
We would need to explore how this might work. For example if we had pre-warning or
if it happened immediately.

Ξ

What skills would be required to do DDR?
We would need at minimum people skilled with the software and computers.
We would need detailed records of the skills and equipment they used, as
what would happen if they left?

Σ
X

How might DDR influence the design of your solution to your issue?
We should investigate how stable our ERP is. Look at a business continuity/
disaster recovery plan. We need to examine what would we do if the ERP
provider would fold. (INSIGHT, a separate Linked Mission which
explores this?) ESCROW?

Θ
Ξ
Φ

Download a blank copy at: *www.changemappingbook.com/advanced-change-mapping-book*

The *Plan* mission

Planning how to resolve an issue

In brief

In this part of the Linked Mission we start to create plans to bring about resolved change, as by this stage we should have evidence that resolving the issue benefits all stakeholders. In our city example, the city council start to plan how to make more skyscrapers have green roofs.

Planning to resolve the issue

This mission is used to plan how you will resolve or address an issue. We strongly recommend not to jump straight to this mission. The preceding missions are used to inform this mission. Without them you will struggle to see how the issue relates to the enterprise it is part of. Are you sure you are resolving the right thing in the most effective way?

Once all of the above is clarified you can use this mission to see what you need to have in place to enact your plan.

Worked example

In our legal firm example the team have run the preceding missions and so have a clear understanding of the big picture and the vision and values of the enterprise they are in. Satisfied they are planning to resolve the right issue in the most effective way, they start to work out the details of who will do the update, who needs to be informed of the update and other considerations. They want to test their plan before updating the ERP software. They will use the next mission, the Test Mission, to test their plan.

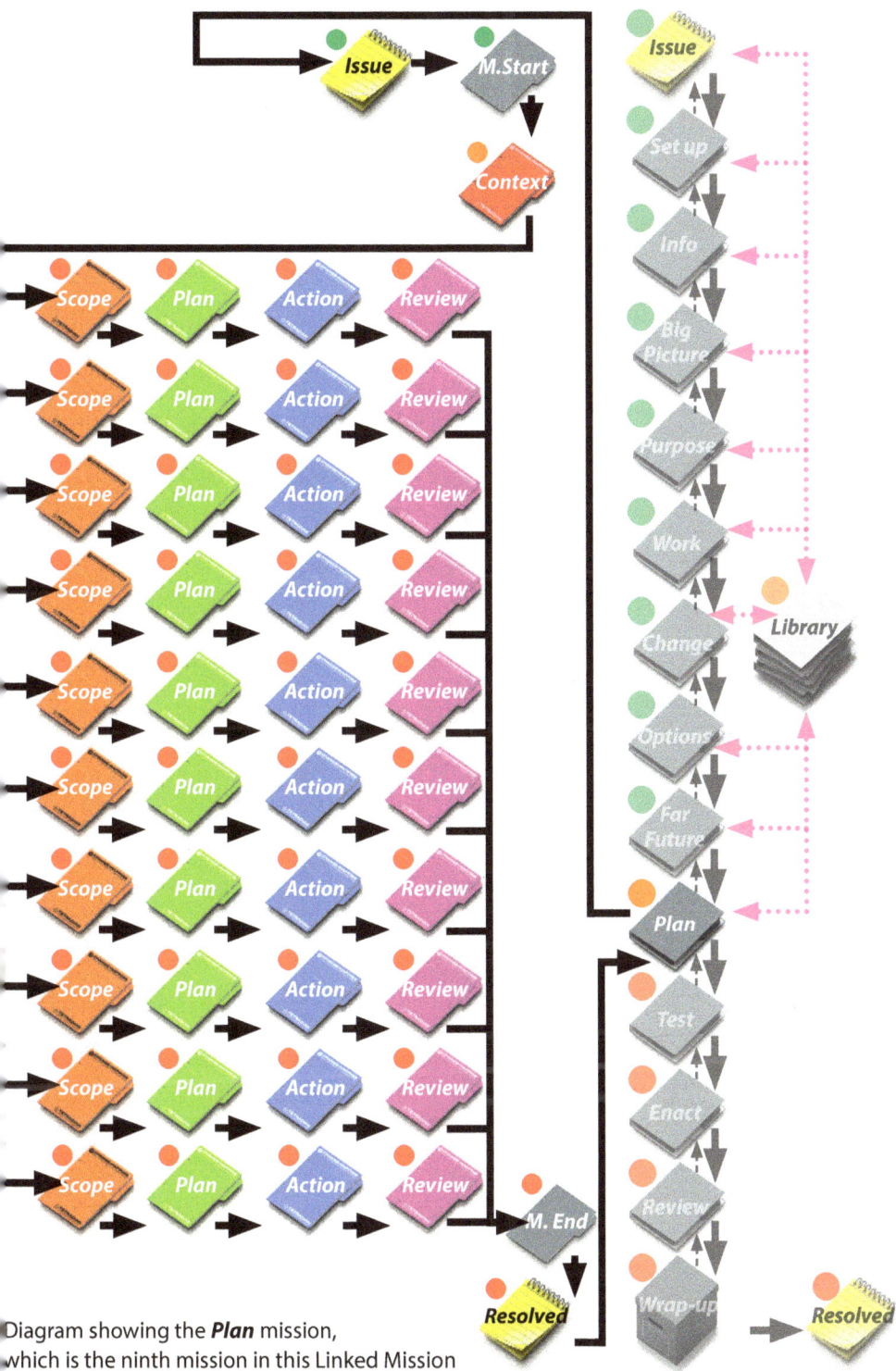

Diagram showing the **Plan** mission,
which is the ninth mission in this Linked Mission

*Using non-Change-mapping
tools in this mission*
*These tools could be used
alongside the questions shown
on the right, to help plan the
resolution of your issue.*
• *AIDA tool*
• *4 Ps tool*
• *Dependencies tools
(What needs to be done and
in what order)*
Further reading
*HM Treasury: Guide to
developing the project
business case*
*HM Treasury: Guide to
developing the programme
business case*
*HM Treasury: The Green Book
Central government guidance
on appraisal and evaluation*

How to use this mission

What is the mission used for?

This mission is used to produce a working plan to resolve
an issue. But it is vital to use the preceding missions to help
shape the plan.

What needs to be done before using this mission tool?

This mission is set-up using standard *Change-mapping (Book
1, page 18)*. Most likely you will be jumping between
missions 6-10 refining your plan, before enacting your plan.

Who is typically involved in this type of mission?

Technical leads, Innovation teams, Process leads/Designers,
Information teams and Enterprise architects.

Warning signs while running the mission

• Submitting to analysis-paralysis *(Book 1, page 54)*.
• Jumping to the plan, without considering future implications
  (see the Far Future mission, page 36).
• Jumping straight to the plan *(Book 1, page 52)*.
• Producing a plan which ignores the vision and values of the
  enterprise you are part of *(see Big Picture Mission, page 16)*.
• Assuming the plan will work *(see Test Mission, page 44)*.
• Not anticipating knock-on effects *(see below)*.

What works well with this mission?

Γ The ***Holomap tool*** *(See Book2, page 22)* used to map out
stakeholders inside an organisation, such as who will be
affected by the issue being resolved.

Λ The ***Effectiveness tool*** *(Book 2, page 34)* to establish effective
approaches to resolving an issue.

Ξ The ***Modes tool*** *(Book 2, page 56)* to assess how best to
approach resolving an issue.

Σ The ***Leadership tool*** *(Book 2, page 48)* to elect leaders who can
make decisions under difficult conditions.

Φ The ***SCORE tool*** *(Book 2, page 74)* to explore what capabilities
your organisation has to resolve the issue.

X The ***Where to start tool*** *(Book 2, page 78)* to explore how to
resolve an unknown issue.

Mission identification: Linked Mission to update our Legal firm's ERP system
20CTOBER2032-MISSION-02048

Mission 9 of 13 *Answer all questions using Change-mapping techniques (Book1, page 18).*

What skills, people, equipment, materials do you need to enact the final plan?
Skills: Familiarity with ERP software, IT systems, Observation
People: IT specialists, test group of stakeholders, observers (to record enactment).
Software, Computers, WI-FI, communication systems.

Γ Χ
Ξ
Σ Φ

How will you partition the enactment? (For example who is doing what, when, where?)
IT will handle the upload of the software and any resulting issues.
Enactment leader will lead the project to update the software.

Χ

What is a breakdown of the tasks needed to enact the plan?
Inform people of the update and promote the benefits. Have a disaster recovery
plan (tested) in place. Make sure all assets are in place before enactment.
Need to have run tests before unleashing the updates.

Χ

What are the dependencies? (For example, what needs to be done first?)
We need to run small scale tests first to see what are the unexpected
consequences and benefits. (INSIGHT> These tests could be in a simulated
version of our operation). Then much as in the question above.

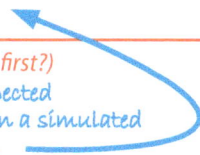

What is the budget for the enactment? (For example costs and timings)
We need to speak to IT what are realistic budgets and time-scales.
(INSIGHT> We should look at budgets for a disaster response team, in case
something happens that no one predicted, but needs solving urgently).

Χ

How do you keep all involved on track? (For example people keep a global focus)
Possibly a project champion and team to keep all affected by the update
informed. And those enacting the plan given all they need including
decisions, as soon as they need things.

What happens if one part of the plan fails, how will it affect all the other parts?
The testing phase should inform what and why something is failing. We
may need to have redundant systems, to allow things to carry on. Such as a
back-up generator, should the main one fail.

Σ

How will you enact the plan? (In stages, in one stage? How long for each stage?)
If we look at page 48 we can see a plan broken down into: Before action,
during action and so on. We will refer to this before final enactment and
informed by what happens in the Test mission (see page 44).

Χ
Ξ

How will the solution be announced, designed, built and stored?
We need to see who are the stakeholders affected by or affecting the ERP
issue resolution. Once we know who they are we can inform them of what the
changes are and how it will benefit them. The solution in this case is software
and would be cloud based.

Γ
Λ

Describe the initial plan you have devised to resolve your issue.
Inform stakeholders. Gather assets. Run small scale ERP upload tests in virtual
environments. Have disaster recovery and roll-back ready. Upload the software.
(INSIGHT> Have an agreed time where the issue is considered RESOLVED).

Γ
Ξ
Σ Φ

The *Test* mission
Testing a plan before enactment

In brief

In this part of the Linked Mission we test our plan in small-scale real world conditions. In our city example, the city council test the planned city-wide green roof project on a couple of green roofs to look at how the plans work in real world conditions.

Testing the plan in real world conditions

If we need to tackle a large and complex issue, **how** we tackle the issue will need to be worked out.

This mission is used to work out who will be doing what in each of the following missions. For example who will be involved with the **Test mission** *(see diagram on the right)*. What resources, people and time will be required?

Exploring all of these aspects of the entire Linked Mission allows forward planning and avoids bias in certain areas. Once you have all of the above examined you should have everything in place to explore and resolve your issue.

Worked example

In our example, the IT team set up test conditions in a virtual environment. They brought in stakeholders who used the current ERP system and let them use the planned update. Then as notes were taken for what they did typically, the IT team then tried to break the system with more extreme scenarios. The information here showed areas which were weak in isolation and areas which connected to each other.

They added modifications to try to strengthen the system. They then ran the tests again to see if the modifications had the desired effect.

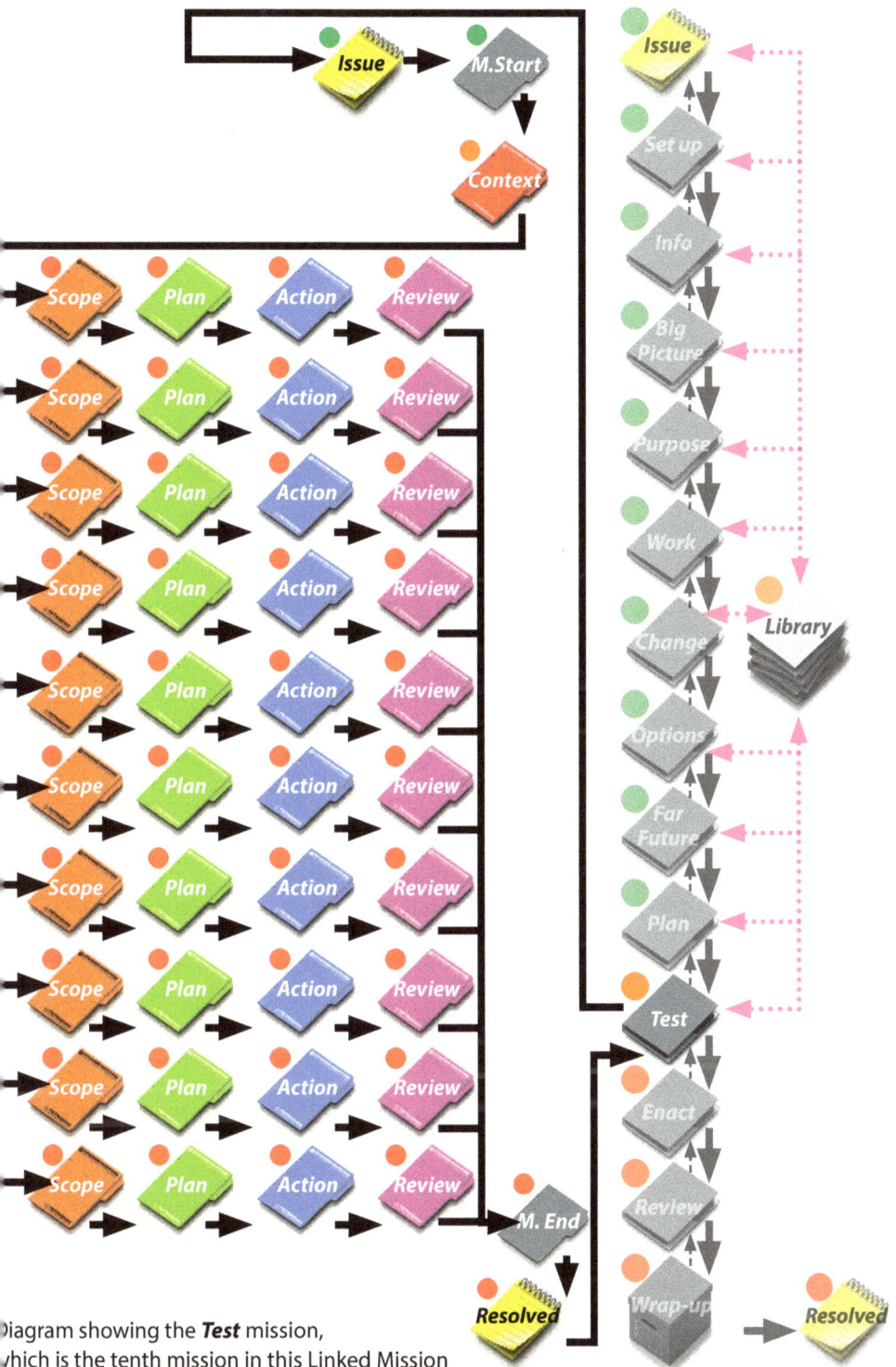

Diagram showing the **Test** mission,
which is the tenth mission in this Linked Mission

How to use this mission

What is the mission used for?

This mission is used to test a plan in real world conditions, before it is enacted in the real world.

What needs to be done before using this mission tool?

This mission is set-up using standard *Change-mapping (Book 1, page 18)*. You will need a basic plan, as this mission is used to try and break that plan in real world conditions.

Who is typically involved in this type of mission?

Test teams, Risk/Opportunity teams, Values teams* and Engineers.
Safety, quality, reliability, sustainability and security (These and others are found in the Enterprise mission).

Warning signs while running the mission

• Testing your planned solution in overly optimistic conditions
• Basing your test conditions on assumptions, rather than gathered evidence.
• Not considering the possibility of uncommon but devastating situations.
• Tests which are impossible to replicate.
• Over-engineering your solution to try to consider every situation.
• Not accepting that there will always be something you didn't think of and submitting to analysis-paralysis.
• Murphy's law: *If something can go wrong, it probably will.*
• Serendipity, sometimes things can just go right for no obvious reason
• Assuming that all parts work.

What works well with this mission?

Δ The **Service cycle tool** can be used to explore where parts could break on the customer journey *(See Book 2, page 30)*.

Θ The **Decision tool** can be used to explore your decision making process in difficult situations *(See Book 2, page 44)*.

Λ The **SEMPER tool** can be used to explore why people feel odd is happening *(See Book 2, page 60)*.

Ξ The **Knock-on effects tool** can be used to look at unexpected consequences of actions *(See Book 2, page 68)*.

Σ The **SCORE tool** can be used to explore how your organisation might resolve an issue *(See Book 2, page 74)*.

Φ The **Where to start tool** can be used to explore how you might resolve an unknown issue *(See Book 2, page 78)*.

X The **SCAN tool** can be used to explore uncertainties surrounding resolving an unknown issue *(See Book 2, page 86)*.

Mission identification: Linked Mission to update our Legal firm's ERP system
20CTOBER2032-MISSION-02048

Mission 10 of 13 *Answer all questions using Change-mapping techniques (Book1, page 18).*

What might cause part of the solution to fail?
Software itself lives in the cloud, connections fail, cloud provider doesn't get our message when to do this and we actually get the old version. Billing or licence issues appear. Δ

What is your back-up plan or Plan B if the solution fails?
Do we have a plan B? What if plan B also doesn't work, some budget for researching alternatives. Bug hunting. We need to make sure cloud people have done what they said they will, don't assume anything! Φ X

How can you test all parts of the solution work together, is there a weakest link?
Deliberately switch bits off and see if software alerts us. Do we have a baseline of what software should be? What if there are extra modules we don't want then we will have to pay? A list of all parts and how they are connected. Θ

If the solution did fail, how would you maintain business continuity?
Deliberately break it. The only people affected are in the testing phase, doesn't actually affect real world. Training needs to be done to prepare people.
What are the things that could have broken and hunt them down and fix them
Intermitent bugs that only happen in special circumstances. Θ Σ

If the solution failed how would you do disaster recovery?
Roll-back, incompatibility when we have a partial roll-backs. Test our roll-backs, version management. Testing our life-raft actually will save us!
What mechanism to identify where the fault happened? Σ

If one part of the solution failed, how would it affect the rest of the solution, ripple effect?
Try to have a modular system, with easily replaceable parts. Redundant parts, in case one part fails then others can adapt. For example, some planes have two engines but can fly on only one. ☰

What happens if one part of the plan fails, how will it affect all the other parts?
Integrators job is to hunt out weak links. For example, one module that can't track physical objects. We want integration with airline shipping is one requirement from us. ☰

If the solution did fail, how would you know that it was failing?
we will set up test examples and see how they work end to end, check not just the software but how it all works and if all parts work together. Place deliberately wrong items to see if they are spotted. Take inspiration from failures in Enact mission; Setup, preflight, in-flight and so on. (See page 48). Λ

What might inform that the solution was failing and overloaded?
we will do stress testing, especially lots of people doing lots of things at once. from multiple countries at same time, synchronisation issues. 1000 messages from Australia and NY at same time then they will arrive or will it break for example? Λ

What are unexpected consequences of the solution failing or succeeding?
Identify the financial, reputation and legal consequences for failure. To what extend are we over engineering a solution and what level of redundancy do we need? Test the level of redundancy required? For example crash barrier not appreciated until they are really needed. ☰

The *Enact* mission
Enacting a plan to resolve an issue

In brief

In this part of the Linked Mission we enact our plan to resolve our issue. For example, our city council now enact the plan to have green roofs on buildings across the city, based on what was found in the testing phase.

Resolving the issue

All the previous missions have lead to this mission.

The teams have asked why does the issue need resolving, should it be resolved and more. By this mission we will have evidence that the issue should be resolved.

This mission uses a set of checklists *(informed by the previous missions)* to assist with resolving the mission.

In addition, we must ensure how the issue is resolved is also recorded. This will be referred to when reviewing the resolution *(the next mission)* and may be vital if people in the future need to recreate or undo what was done *(see page 36)*.

Worked example

In our legal team example, they feel ready to update their ERP (which will resolve their issue). They have pre-flight checklists, people likely to be affected have been informed and other checklists to help resolve the issue. The IT specialist nervously starts the update, first as a small-scale update. They carefully monitor how the update behaves, and after an agreed time they scale up the update.

They refer to their checklists in real time to gauge if any issues are starting to appear. For example, where a few people complain that suddenly fonts are acting strangely.

As the update takes place, an Observer notes the exact details of how the update was done, as this record will help find the cause of any issues.

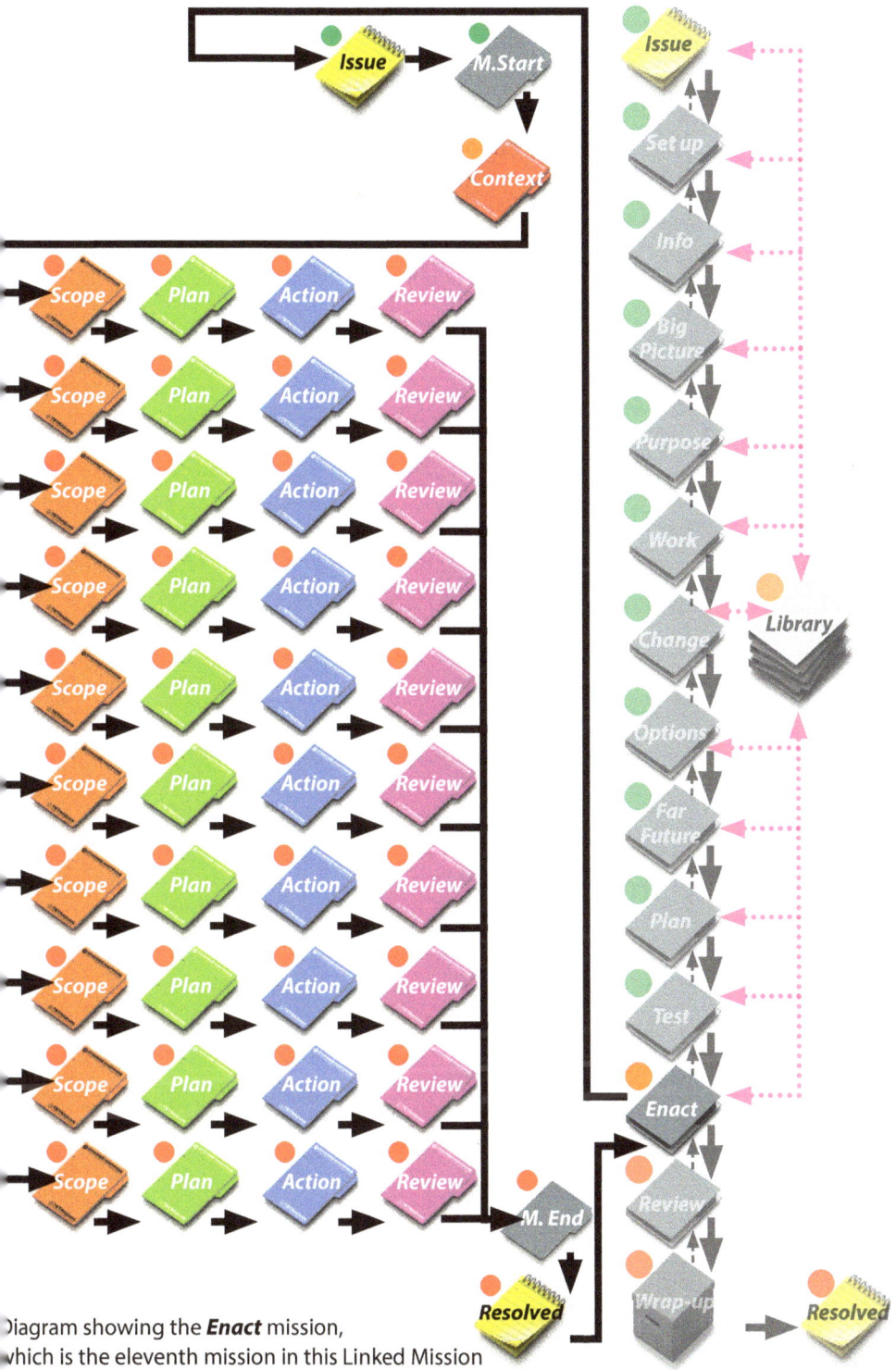

Diagram showing the **Enact** mission,
which is the eleventh mission in this Linked Mission

Using non-Change-mapping tools in this mission

• *Communications checklists*
  This would look at setting up effective lines of communication.
• *Preflight checklists*
• *Start-up checklists*
• *In-flight checklists*
• *Landing checklists*
• *Post flight checklists*
These tools would be used before starting an action; as an action was started; while an action is ongoing; when the action is about to be completed; and after the action has been completed. The last checklist especially would look at clean-up.

How to use this mission

What is the mission used for?

This mission is used to assist and record the resolution of an issue, as it is being resolved. For example, if you plan to build a factory, this would be used during the construction.

What needs to be done before using this mission tool?

This mission is set up using standard *Change-mapping (Book 1 page 18)*. You will need a detailed plan which will be referred to during the enactment of the plan.

Who is typically involved in this type of mission?

This will be the team tasked with the actual resolving of the issue, such as an IT team. There should also be observers who will record the enactment taking place, preferably somebody who is familiar with how to enact the task.

Warning signs while running the mission

• The enactment is differing significantly from your plan.
• Lack of effective leadership.
• Panic *(this should be avoided if the plan was tested in real world conditions, see Test mission, page 44)*
• Blindly following the plan, with no ability to adapt.
• Lack of real-time information between those enacting the plan and those who are decision-makers.
• Poor lines of communication
• Unclear definition of when the issue is considered solved.

What works well with this mission?

Γ *Learning deliverables* are used to record how an issue was resolved *(See page 74 for more details)*.

Δ *Warnings signs* these should have come from the *Testing Mission* *(see page 44)*.

Θ A prepared *Plan*. This will have been created in the earlier missions *(see page 40)*.

nact mission tool

CHANGE→MAPPING
CONNECTING BUSINESS TOOLS TO MANAGE CHANGE

ission identification: Linked Mission to update our Legal firm's ERP system
20CTOBER2032-MISSION-02048

Mission 11 of 13 *Answer all questions using Change-mapping techniques (Book1, page 18).*

Do you have start-up plans for your enactment?
We have a set of start-up plans. We will upload the updated ERP in just one
department which will send the update to the second department. We will use
an allotted time period to see if unexpected problems occur. Θ

Do you have the ability to record the enactment taking place?
We are documenting each stage of the process, we have an observer (Book 1,
page 12) taking notes and screen-grabbing the computer. We also have an
observer at the other end, to compare. Γ Θ

Is the plan working in real world conditions?
The plan seems to be working at present, but we need to wait the allotted time
in case unexpected events appear. Δ

Is the equipment, materials and location working as expected?
Generally the software is working as expected, but the fonts are acting in an
unexpected way, which we never predicted...

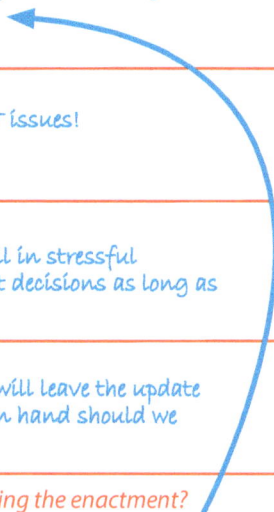

Do the people enacting the mission have the right skills?
Our IT people have many years experience and used to IT issues! Λ

Is there good leadership?
Our COO doesn't have much IT experience but works well in stressful
conditions and we trust him to be able to make difficult decisions as long as
he has real time information.

Is there sufficient information in real time?
We are monitoring the update in real time and then we will leave the update
and review it before scaling up the update. The COO is on hand should we
have to pull the plug.

Are there unexpected events (good or bad) happening during the enactment?
The fonts were an issue, but the IT dept. contacted the vendor who gave us
advice about how to fix the small issue. We have noticed the computer is using
more computing power than normal, which we are monitoring.

What is the sign that the issue is resolved?
After a week we judged the update to be 99% successful and will start to scale
up the update.

Is the issue staying resolved?
After a month the update was for the most part successful.
We are monitoring any complaints and have a roll-back in place
should it be required.

The *Review* mission
Was the issue successfully resolved?

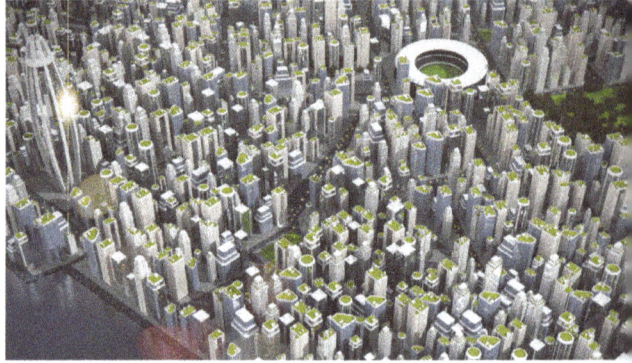

In brief

In this part of the Linked Mission we review if the issue was successfully resolved. To resolve the issue overall may involve lots of smaller Nested Missions (See Book 1, page 114) which need planning, enacting and reviewing, before the main issue can be resolved. In our city example, there are now many skyscrapers with green roofs. But first they had to set up approved construction standards, contractors and more, before building the green roofs. Then once the standards were set up they could then actually convert the roofs to become green spaces.

Did we resolve our issue?

After the issue has been resolved, this mission is used to review how successful the enactment was. Was the plan followed effectively and did the plan work well in the real world? A large amount of these questions will be answered with evidence gathered in the **Enact** mission *(see page 48)*. Here your team will compare the notes from the **Enact** mission with questions posed in this mission. The review may take place months after the enactment, as it may take a set period to see if an issue is truly resolved and stays resolved.

Worked example

In our legal firm example, the review took place a month after the new ERP software was installed. This gave them a reasonable amount of time to see if the update was successful. Part of this was a NESTED MISSION (see Book 1, page 114) where there were weekly interviews with key stakeholders. These interviews involved asking if any issues were starting to appear and collate that information for first fixing said issues and secondly for the review.

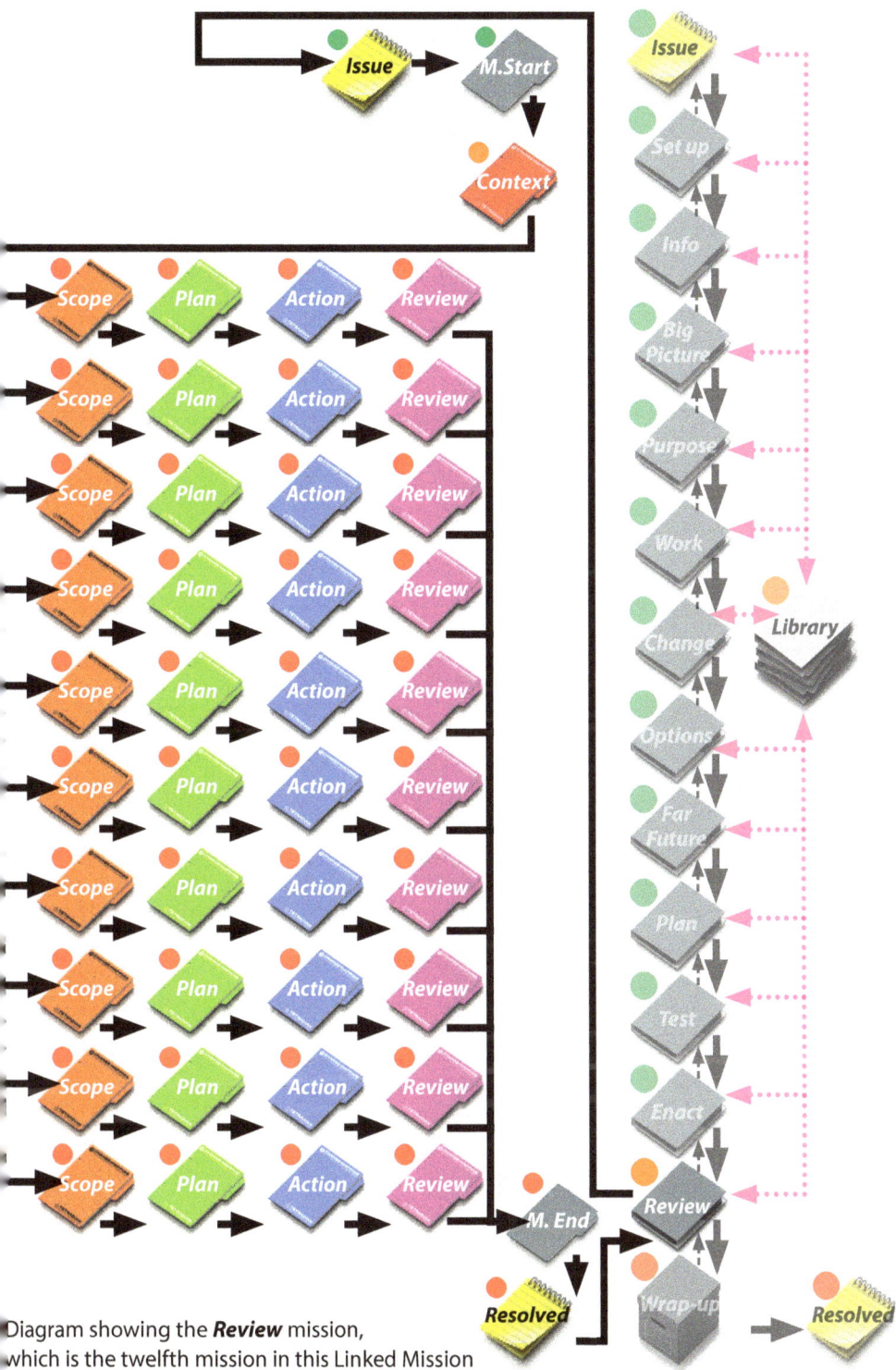

Diagram showing the **Review** mission,
which is the twelfth mission in this Linked Mission

*Using non-Change-mapping
tools in this mission*
• After Action Review
• Performance appraisal
• Project review
*These tools could be used
alongside the questions shown
on the right, to help review
how the plan
was enacted.*
Further reading
*UK Government:
Project assurance reviews
delivery confidence guide
for review teams*

Extra information
*The red box will likely be filled
out at an earlier date than the
dashed section of the tool,
shown on the right.*

How to use this mission

What is the mission used for?

This mission is used to review the enactment of a plan.
For example, was the outcome successful and what
was learnt?

What needs to be done before using this mission tool?

This mission is set up using standard *Change-mapping
(Book 1, page 18)*. You will have recorded a plan being enacted.
This recording will form the basis of the review. You will need
to pre-decide when the Review mission will take place.

Who is typically involved in this type of mission?

Project leads, Stakeholders affected by the enactment, the
team that enacted the plan, Enterprise architects *(to cross-
check that the vision and values were not compromised)*.

Warning signs while running the mission

• Not following the plan properly.
• Making the facts fit your theory.
• Not learning from what happened and repeating the
  same mistakes.
• Forgetting that everyone is responsible, not just those
  enacting the plan.
• Shifting blame, evading responsibility
• Reviewing without detailed records *(for example from the
  Enact mission, see page 48)*

What works well with this mission?

Γ The **Basic Review tool** *(Book1, Page 94)* to assist basic reviews.

Δ The **Holomap tool** *(Book 2, page 22)* to cross-check that all
  stakeholders felt the issue was resolved effectively.

Θ The information gathered in the preceding missions, such as
  the **Big Picture Mission** *(see page 16)*.

Λ It can be useful to cross-check with what was found in the
  Far Future Mission *(see page 36)*.

Ξ The **Knock-on effects tool** can be useful to look at
  unexpected effects of resolving the issue. *(Book 2, page 68)*.

Σ The **SEMPER tool** helps establish if staff feel they can
  function effectively. *(Book 2, page 60)*.

Mission identification: Linked Mission to update our Legal firm's ERP system
20CTOBER2032-MISSION-02048

Mission 12 of 13 *Answer all questions using Change-mapping techniques (Book 1, page 18).*

How long after the issue is resolved will the review take place?
This review took place one month after the ERP software update.
We agreed that this gave enough time for unexpected issues to appear.
Γ Θ

How was the issue successfully resolved?
The ERP software update we feel for the most part was successfully resolved.
Apart from a small amount of problems, the update is working as expected.
Γ Θ

How was the plan effective or did you have to adapt the plan?
We felt the plan was as worked out as it could be, some of the unexpected
events (such as font issues) although not anticipated were easy to fix, as we
had planned for those kinds of problems.
Γ Θ

How did you stay true to the enterprise's and organisation's vision and values?
We feel after checking through the preceding missions that we stayed true to
the vision and values. For example the Effectiveness tool (Book 2, page 34)
mentions: Appropriate. Our solution was appropriate to us and the enterprise.
Θ

How might the enactment change if it was scaled up?
We deliberately kept the enactment small, before doing the company-wide
ERP update. A company-wide update will involve informing a lot more
people, more variables and require more time, for example.
Ξ

What would you do differently if the enactment was repeated?
If we were to repeat the update at the same scale, we maybe BEFORE the
enactment would try some harsher real world scenarios to see how the update
might behave.
Λ

How have stakeholders embraced the change brought about by the issue's resolution?
There was some resistance to the change but most stakeholders are happy
with the new ERP update. We also ran a NESTED MISSION to gather
stakeholder's views every week acting as focus groups, reviewing the update.
Σ

How did the equipment, materials and location perform during the enactment?
The software and hardware all worked as predicted. We had a slight delay
when communicating with different users, but this didn't affect
anything significantly.
Γ Θ

How did the people involved with the enactment perform?
Our IT team worked well and were on hand to remedy problems.
They also kept stakeholders aware of the update.
Γ

Describe if there was enough time, money and information available.
We would have preferred more time for testing. We would have liked to
have been consulted when the time-scales were considered. The budget was
sufficient for the update.
Γ Θ Δ

The *Wrap-up* mission
Reviewing the Linked Mission

In brief

In this part of the Linked Mission we review the entire Linked Mission and decide what, if anything, needs to be done next. One example might be to make sure that the issue stays resolved.

In our city example, while the issue raised was to have a more sustainable city, having green skyscraper roofs was only part of that ultimate goal. The city would then start to tackle some other areas to make the city more sustainable.

What have we learnt?

If we need to tackle a large and complex issue, **how** we tackle the issue will need to be worked out.

This mission is used to work out who will be doing what in each of the following missions. For example who will be involved with the **Test mission** *(see diagram on the right)*. What resources, people and time will be required?

Exploring all of these aspects of the entire Linked Mission allows forward planning and avoids bias in certain areas.

Once you have all of the above examined you should have everything in place to explore and resolve your issue.

Worked example

In our example the ERP update was successfully updated in a small scale staggered roll-out. The Linked Mission was seen as helping establish the rationale behind the update and helping facilitate the successful resolution of the issue.

The Linked Mission was made up of thirteen missions which themselves often had Nested Missions inside them.

The Wrap-up mission was used to review all of those missions and how they interacted with each other.

Another part that was investigated was how the Library was used to share information found in the ERP Linked Mission and supplied to other Linked Missions. For example, while our team concentrated on the issue surrounding ERP systems our colleagues were concentrating on the Enterprise (in general). This information they found, was useful to us in our Linked Mission.

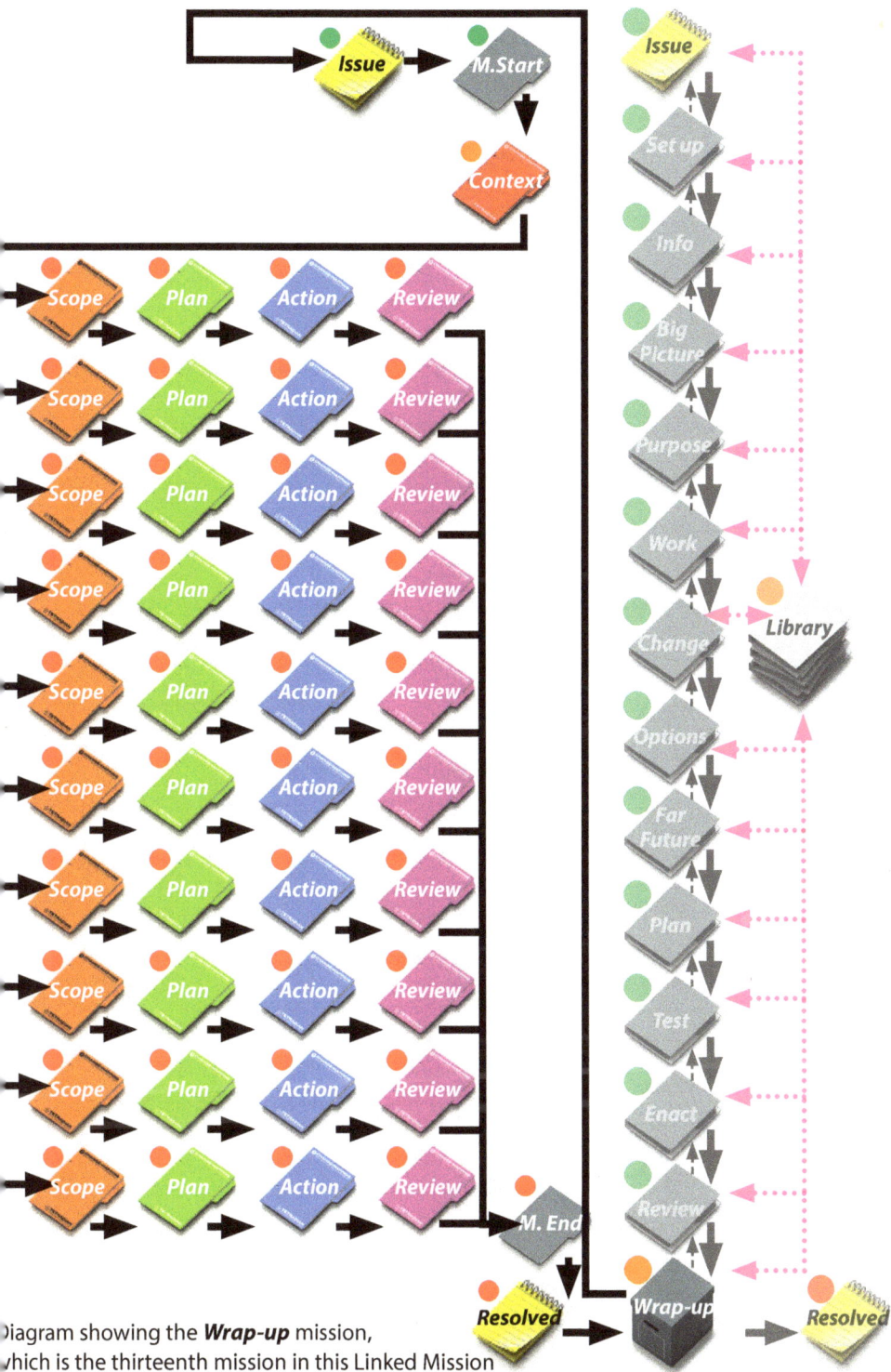

Diagram showing the **Wrap-up** mission,
which is the thirteenth mission in this Linked Mission

Further reading
*UK Government:
Project assurance reviews
delivery confidence guide
for review teams*

Extra information
The red box will likely be filled out at an earlier date than the dashed section of the tool, shown on the right.

How to use this mission
What is the mission used for?
This mission is used to review the *entire* Linked Mission, whereas the Review Mission would be used to review one part. For example, a Linked Mission to resolve building a bridge, would be made up of many parts, each part having its own Review mission.

What needs to be done before using this mission tool?
This mission is set-up using standard *Change-mapping (Book 1, page 18)*. You will need access to all parts of the Linked Mission, this will be accessed from your own mission notes and relevant Library files. You will need to pre-decide when the Wrap-up mission will take place.

Who is typically involved in this mission?
A cross-section of all involved in the Linked Mission, such as Project leads, Stakeholders affected by the enactment, the team that enacted the plan, Enterprise architects *(to cross-check that the vision and values were not compromised)*.

Warning signs while running the mission
• Making the facts fit your theory.
• Not learning from what happened and repeating the same mistakes.
• Forgetting that everyone is responsible, not just those enacting plans.

What works well with this mission?
Γ The **Basic Review tool** *(Book1, Page 94)* to assist basic reviews.

Δ The **Holomap tool** *(Book 2, page 22)* to cross-check that all stakeholders felt the issue was resolved effectively.

Θ The information gathered in the preceding missions, such as the **Big Picture Mission** *(see page 16)*.

Λ It can be useful to cross-check with what was found in the **Far Future Mission** *(see page 36)*.

☰ The **Knock-on effects tool** can be useful to look at unexpected effects of resolving the issue. *(Book 2, page 68)*.

Σ The **SEMPER tool** helps establish if staff feel they can function effectively with the issue resolved. *(Book 2, page 60)*.

Any any of the tools mentioned in this part of the book could also be reused to gauge how things are now after the change, compared to before. For example, a customer journey review could compare how the customer journey has changed after the issue has been resolved.

Wrap-up mission tool

CHANGE→MAPPING
CONNECTING BUSINESS TOOLS TO MANAGE CHANGE

Mission identification: Linked Mission to update our Legal firm's ERP system.
20OCTOBER2032-MISSION-02048

Mission 13 of 13 *Answer all questions using Change-mapping techniques (Book 1, page 18).*

How long after the issue is resolved will the Linked Mission review take place?
We will do this review of the entire Linked Mission three months after the
ERP system update.

Γ Θ

How was the issue successfully resolved?
The IT team did multiple test runs in virtual environments. These tests
highlighted problems when the system became overloaded. We consulted with the
software provider who created a patch to remedy this part of the overall issue.

Γ Δ

How effective was the Linked Mission?
It worked in stages: 1 Why were doing the update? 2 What were our best
options and 3 Testing that our option would actually work. These and other
stages helped us see where we were in the issue.

Γ Θ

How did you stay true to the enterprise's vision and values?
We stayed focused on our issue and the overall enterprise. We did this with
the help of the Library, who supplied information (created by others) about
the enterprise.

Γ Θ Λ

How might the enactment change if it was scaled up?
We feel that a modular approach with redundancy built in would work for us.
The virtual environment could be upgraded to test scaling up the ERP update.
Some of this is still unknown and would need its own Linked Mission?

Γ Θ Ξ

What would you do differently if the enactment was repeated?
We had assumed a lot about what the vendor would do. We would, if repeating, have
a dedicated liaison between us and the vendor. Also bringing in the vendor more
into the virtual environment.

Γ Θ Ξ Λ

How have stakeholders embraced the change brought about by the issue's resolution?
Mostly, there was a "If it's not broken why fix it?" view. But people are
starting to see the benefits. Especially the working from home benefits, with
full connectivity to the ERP.

Γ Δ Σ

How did the equipment, materials and location perform during the enactment?
Most of the equipment worked well. Our WIFI did start to act oddly at one
point, which was due to the manufacturer updating their software! They
hadn't told us they were doing this, which gave the IT team problems!

Γ Θ

How did the people involved with the enactment perform?
Most people were fully committed. Some of our clients were dubious about why they
needed to be involved in testing, but once we started they changed their opinions.
The IT department went above and beyond to get the update working on time.

Γ Θ Σ

Describe if there was enough time, money and information available.
We could always to with more time, money and information. But there
comes a point where we have to just do something! See Book 1, page 54 about
analysis-paralysis.

Γ Θ

An issue is resolved
The end of a *Linked Mission*?

About this page in brief
Here we look at what happens
(if anything) after a
Linked Mission.

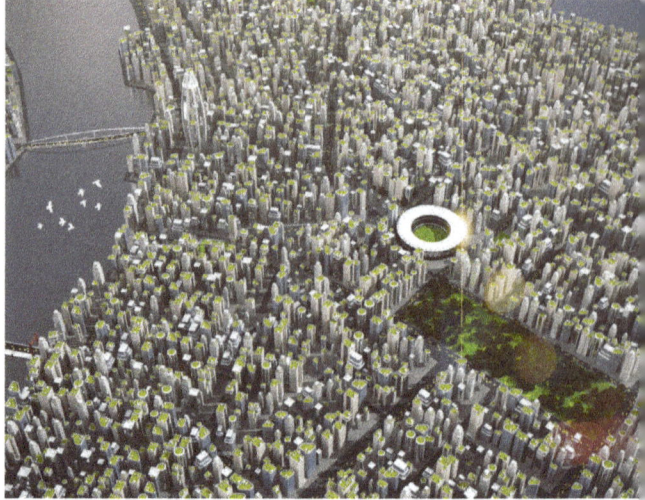

What happens next

Often, quite reasonably, people are focused on resolving an issue and nothing else. But what happens after the issue is resolved? Sometimes people can lose motivation, once they have managed to achieve their goal. Other times effort is required to *keep* an issue resolved which can become a mission in itself. Another important point is to celebrate that you have achieved your goal and praise those involved for all their efforts. In the next part of the book we will look at some other, more specialised missions, which can support a Linked Mission.

Worked example

In our example the ERP system update has been successful. Now the legal firm decides that they want to scale up the ERP system update across all their offices globally. They decide to run a Scale-up mission (another Linked Mission) to explore the challenges and opportunities might arise.
They also decide to explore a few other issues, indirectly related to ERP, that were discovered while trying to resolve the ERP update.

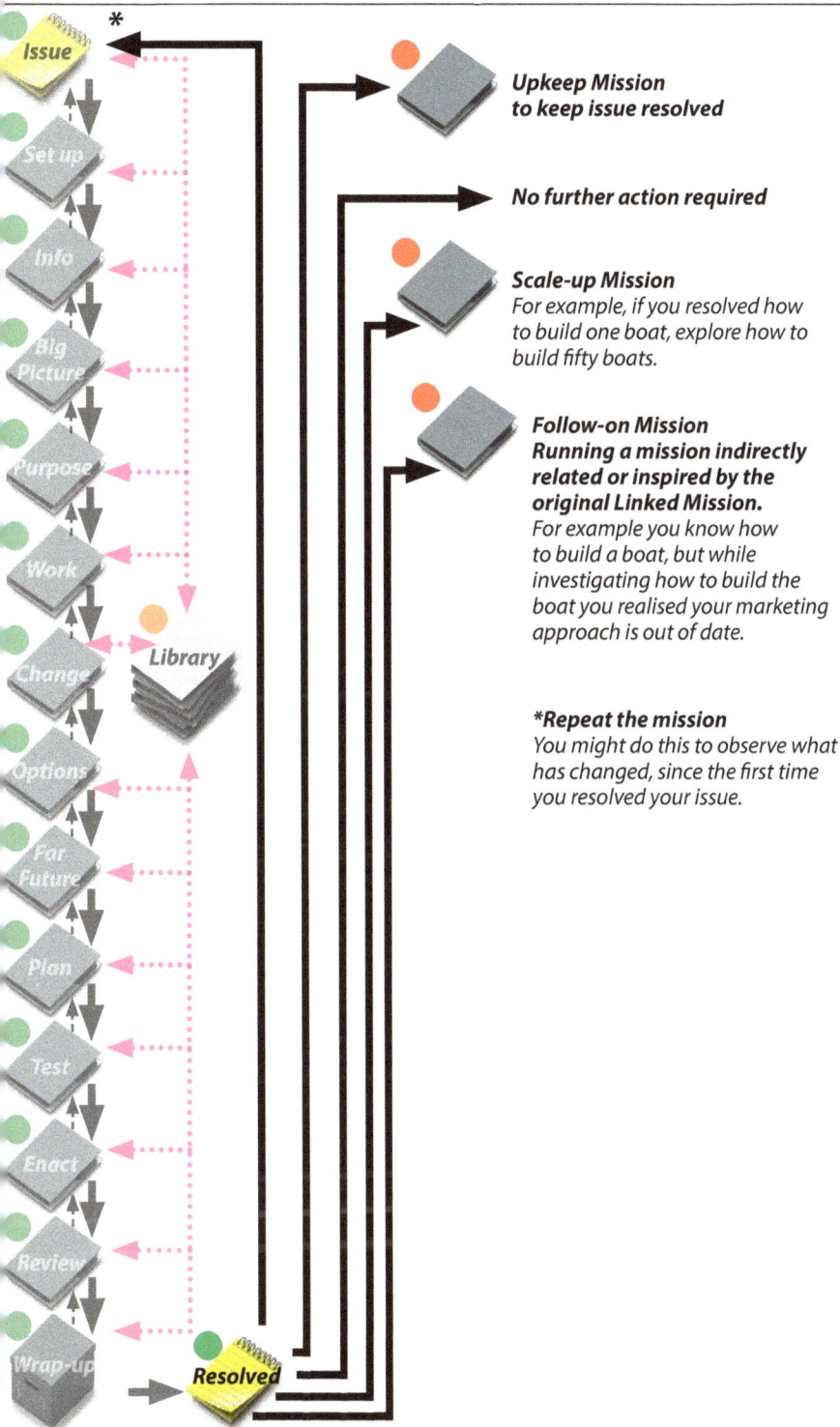

Issue *

Set up

Info

Big Picture

Purpose

Work

Change

Library

Options

Far Future

Plan

Test

Enact

Review

Wrap-up

Resolved

Upkeep Mission
to keep issue resolved

No further action required

Scale-up Mission
For example, if you resolved how to build one boat, explore how to build fifty boats.

Follow-on Mission
Running a mission indirectly related or inspired by the original Linked Mission.
For example you know how to build a boat, but while investigating how to build the boat you realised your marketing approach is out of date.

*Repeat the mission
You might do this to observe what has changed, since the first time you resolved your issue.

Diagram showing some possible options after the Linked Mission has ended

Part 2:
How to get more from *Linked Missions*

While Linked Missions are used to tackle a specific issue, there are other missions that need to run in the background. These will help you better understand the context of your issue and share that information. In this part of the book we look at some of these and other types of missions.

What is a Library Mission?

Sharing and storing information effectively

CGI Joseph Chittenden

Deliverables from a Library mission
The main parts which will be needed for the Library are how to: Save, Categorise, Distribute, Archive, Delete, Secure, Update, Recreate and Migrate your Change-mapping information.

An overview

In the previous part of the book, we looked at how a Linked mission could be used to tackle large and complex issues. In that part, the importance of having an effective Library was mentioned. Here we look at the Library in more detail. A Library of information will be vital to make sure that the right information gets to the right people at the right time.

How does a Library Mission compare to a Linked Mission?

The diagram on the right shows how a Library Mission is really just another Linked Mission *(see page 4)*. It is set up and run just like any other Linked Mission. Its issue to be explored and resolved is: ***How do we store and share information for Change-mapping missions inside our organisation?***
You would work through the missions so that you have a Library ready to store and share information. The only real difference is that as the Library will always be needed, so the Wrap-up mission is now changed to an Upkeep mission.
In brief an Upkeep mission *(see page 68)* is used to maintain a product or service, such as the organisation's Library.
When we say a Library, it may not be one library. It might be a collection of linked places, some storing data while others store physical artefacts.
On page 72 we show some roles which could be used to run a Library. For example the people who ***set up*** the Library might be quite different to the ones who ***run*** the Library. The running of the Library is practically a service and so is managed with an ***Upkeep*** mission *(see page 68)*.

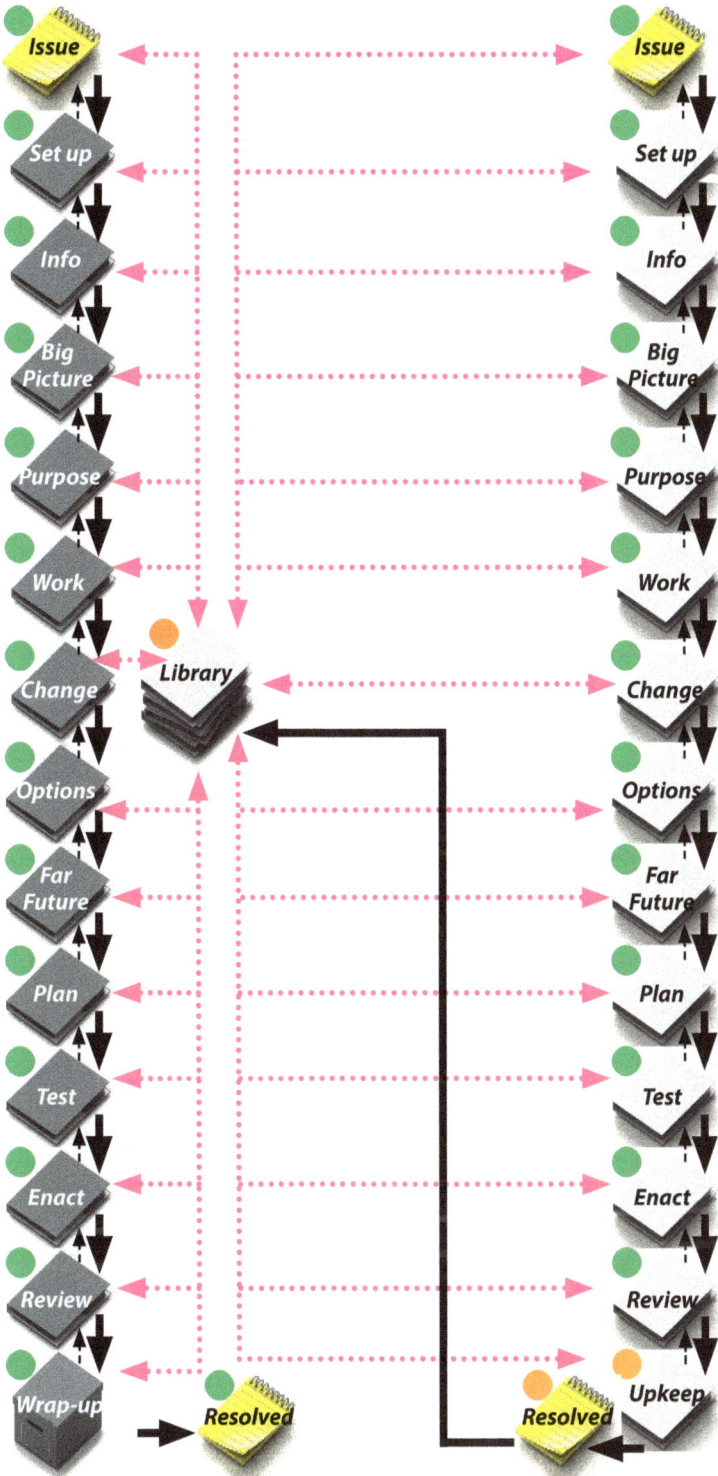

Diagram showing a typical Linked Mission

Diagram showing a typical Library Mission

What is an Enterprise Mission?

Understanding the big picture

More about the enterprise
Page 16 shows a Big Picture
Mission which covers most of
what is needed in an
Enterprise Mission.

Book1, page 68 has a basic
context tool-sheet.

Book 2, page 4 has a chapter
describing a set of context
tools. These are
used to:
Measure value
Proceed with limited
information
Define an organisation
Map an organisation's services
Map stakeholders
Guide an organisation
See the customer's journey
Be more effective

An overview

In the Linked Mission part of the book we discussed how a Library would need to be used to share and store information. A large amount of this information would be generated in a different Linked Mission exploring the enterprise that your organisation is part of.

The Enterprise Linked Mission would be always running in the background, supplying context information *(via the Library)* to any Linked Mission which needed it. We can see this working on page 16. There a team is exploring ERP and needs to understand the enterprise, but don't have time to explore it themselves, so they use Enterprise information created by the Enterprise Linked Mission and sourced from the Library.

How does an Enterprise Mission compare to a Linked Mission?

The diagram on the right shows how an Enterprise Mission is really just another Linked Mission *(See page 4)*. Its issue to be explored and resolved is: ***How can we understand the enterprise which our organisation is part of?***

You would work through the missions *(shown right)* so that you have Enterprise information ready to send to the Library. The only real difference is that as this mission never ends, so the ***Wrap-up*** mission is now changed to an ***Upkeep*** mission. In brief an Upkeep mission *(see page 68)* is used to maintain a product or service, such as the organisation's Library.

One new role introduced on page 72 is the architect who would most likely be heavily involved with the Enterprise mission, gathering information about the enterprise. Part of that role would be observing patterns between various parts of the enterprise and avoiding single focus *(see page 88)*.

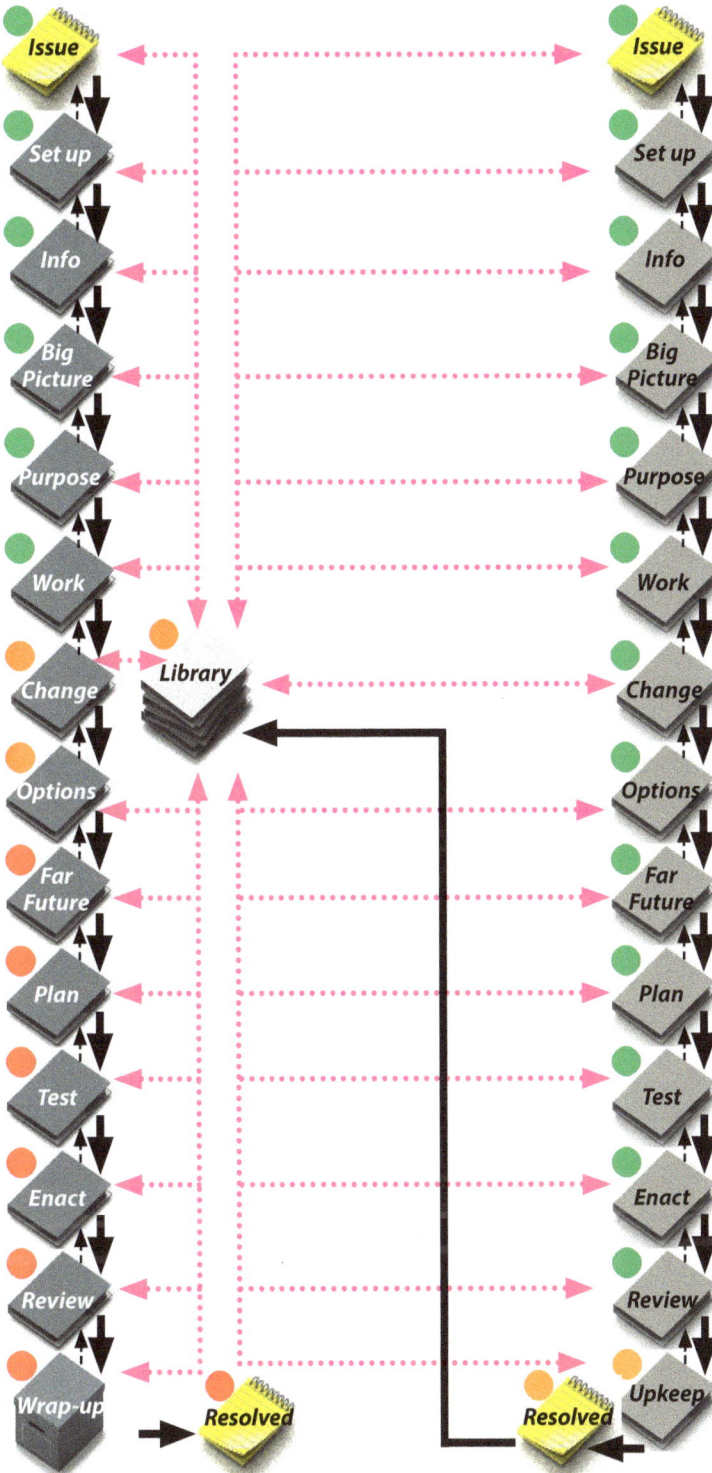

Diagram showing a typical inked Mission

Diagram showing a typical Enterprise Mission

The *Upkeep* mission
Maintaining a service or product

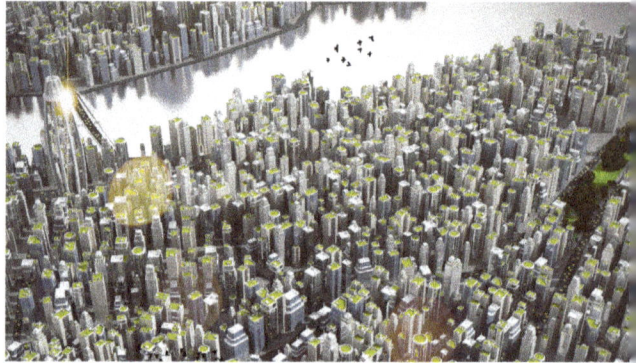

In brief

This mission replaces a
Wrap-up Mission *(see page 56) and is used to maintain a product or service.*
In our city example, there are skyscrapers with green roofs, but they need to be maintained to stop them falling into disrepair.

Making sure things stay resolved

The focus of the main Linked Mission is to explore and usually resolve or address an issue. But often the issue has a habit of unresolving itself. Or it needs to be maintained to make sure it works as efficiently as possible. There are various ways this can be tackled using *Change-mapping*. You could start a new Linked Mission where the issue raised is to maintain a service or product. Or, as shown here, have a mission inside a Linked Mission which does the same thing. The second example is a Upkeep mission. It works exactly like any other mission except its focus is on maintenance.

Worked example

In our legal firm example, the IT team need to keep the ERP system running smoothly. They decide to use a Upkeep mission to help do this. The Upkeep mission is split into key areas. Some of these include allowing those who have been tasked with maintaining the ERP system full access to the original Linked Mission notes. This will help them see what is going on and why, rather than wasting time guessing why something has been set-up in a certain way.
Another area is to look at what and who is needed to maintain our ERP system.
Another area which has been forgotten in the past is asking the awkward question of what circumstances might say that we shouldn't maintain our ERP system. There can be a temptation to say it must work whatever happens, but not at the expense of staff safety for example. We need to look at those risks (again as we explored them in the Testing mission) and try to get around those risks without affecting staff safety in any way.

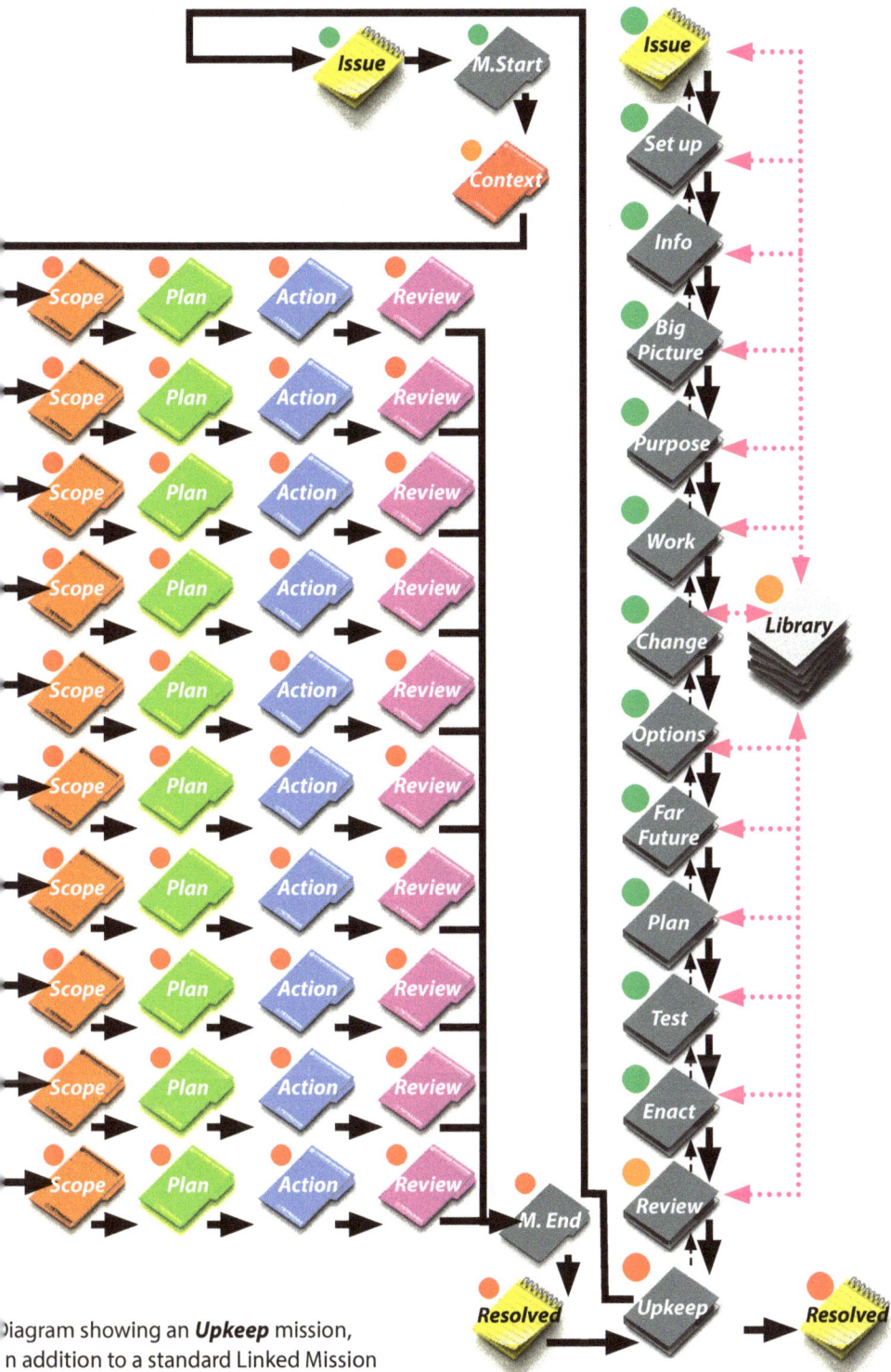

Diagram showing an **Upkeep** mission, in addition to a standard Linked Mission

Using non-Change-mapping tools in this mission

- Data logs
- Quality standards
- Risk management
- Maintenance standards
- Following standard procedures

These tools could be used alongside the questions shown on the right, to help review how the plan was enacted.

Further reading

UK Government:
Project assurance reviews
delivery confidence guide
for review teams

How to use this mission

What is the mission used for?

This mission is used to maintain an existing product or service

What needs to be done before using this mission tool?

This mission is set up using standard *Change-mapping* (Book 1, page 18). Typically you will have run a Linked Mission to set up a product or service. At other times you may be maintaining somebody else's product or service. In either case, working with the Library should help you assess what is going on and why.

Who is typically involved in this type of mission?

Stakeholders who are invested in maintaining the product or service. The *Change-mapping* Library to share information. The actual people who will maintain the product or service, which could range from engineers to rangers, depending on the particular circumstances.

Warning signs while running the mission

- Ignoring warning signs.
- Making the facts fit your theory.
- Not learning from what happened and repeating the same mistakes.
- Failing to do preventive maintenance.
- Failing to understand when it's not worth maintaining the product or service.
- Refusing to accept that you may have to stop maintenance. (Your purpose must align with the enterprise).

What works well with this mission?

Γ The best source of information should be the notes from the Linked Mission which was used to set up the product or service.

Δ The *Decision tool* helps explore how your organisation makes decisions. (Book 2, page 44).

Θ The *Modes tool* helps explore the types of team you might want to maintain a product or service. (Book 2, page 56).

Λ The *SEMPER tool* helps establish if staff feel they can function effectively. (Book 2, page 60).

Ξ The *Knock-on effects tool* explores the possible consequences of maintaining or not maintaining a product or service. (Book 2, page 68).

Mission identification: Linked Mission to update our Legal firm's ERP software
20CTOBER2032-MISSION-02048

Special Mission *Answer all questions using Change-mapping techniques (Book1, page 18).*

What is the product or service that needs to be maintained and why?
Our legal firm's ERP system which was updated recently to version 2.
Apart from the cost to update the ERP, the obvious need to keep it running.
Otherwise why did we update the ERP? Γ

What should the product or service be doing, when working well?
Some examples include: Having our legal team in the right place at the right
time. Having legal documents in the right place at the right time. Γ Λ

What do you have in place to tell you when it isn't working well?
We have set up monitoring systems and also the stakeholders are not shy
to tell us when things are not working! Γ Λ

How are you monitoring the product/service for potential issues?
Yes, we have a dedicated team who monitor the IT systems and keep in
contact with key stakeholders.

What might cause the product/service to fail?
We explored this in-depth in the Test mission. One example might be an
overload of the system, such as a vast amount of people using the system at
the same time. Γ ☰

What redundancies do you have to keep the product/service going in difficult conditions?
Again we explored this in the Test mission. One example is that we have a dedicated
contact with the ERP vendor to resolve issues quickly before they get out of control
(INSIGHT> Mission to explore when issues are likely to explode?) Γ ☰

At what point would you decide to not maintain the product or service?
The most obvious is if there was a danger to anyone maintaining the service.
We have explored the risks involved, such as fire or sensitive information
getting into the wrong hands. Δ ☰

What equipment is required to maintain the product or service?
We have specified this in the Linked Mission, as there are large amounts
of equipment required. Γ

Which people and skills are required to maintain the product or service?
Again this was specified in the Linked Mission used to set up the ERP
system update. Γ Θ

Describe if there is enough time, money and information available?
We feel that there is not enough of a realistic budget for time or money to
properly maintain the ERP service in certain conditions. Some management
have ignored our views on Kurtosis risk (see page 104)

Other types of Support Missions
Linked Missions to help other Linked Missions

CGI Joseph Chittenden

Asking the right questions
On the right are some suggestions of Linked Missions which can be used to support any Linked Mission you run. Part 3 of this book looks at some areas which can become major issues if ignored.

An overview

A Linked Mission can be run independently to explore, resolve or address an issue such as managing a vineyard.

But as we have shown, some Linked Missions are used to support other Linked missions, such as the Enterprise Mission. There are multiple Support Linked Missions which could be run, which allow you to go into great detail, without losing track of where and why you are exploring an issue.

Some examples of Support Linked Missions

This list suggests some potential subjects which could be explored in your support Linked Missions.
- Explore your organisation's purpose
- How your organisation functions *(see Book 2, page 38)*
- Rules and regulations of the enterprise
- Risk *(see Book 2, page 74 SCORE. Also this book, page 104)*
- Trust and stakeholders *(see page 84)*
- Sustainability and the circular economy
- Business ethics
- Avoiding bias or singular focus *(see page 88)*
- Business architecture *(see page 92)*
- Health and safety
- Financial probity
- Looking at the long term rather than short term
- Security
- Strategy
- Facilities management
- Mental welfare of staff *(see page 108)*
- Products and services *(see page 96)*
- Best practices *(see page 100)*

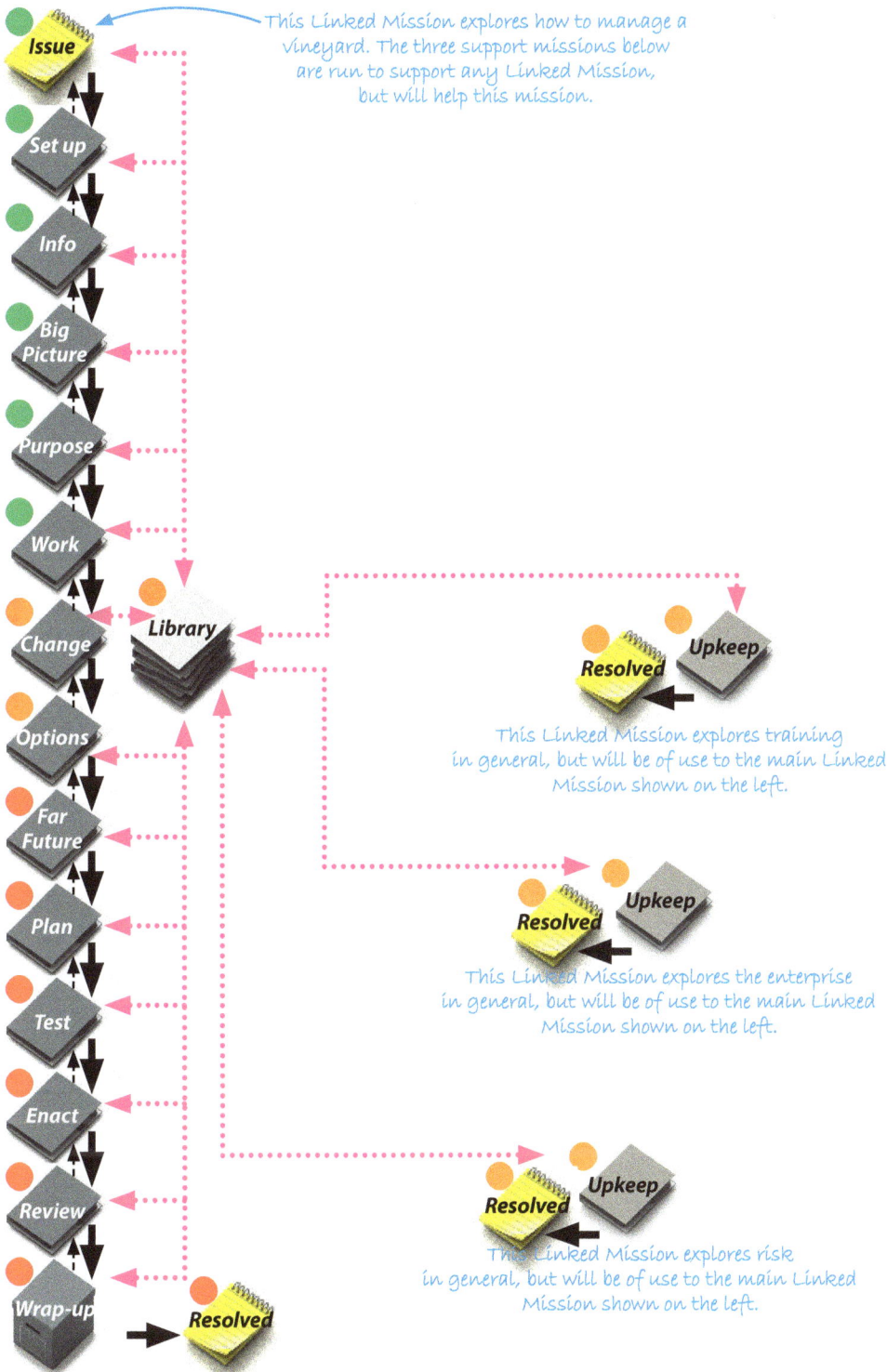

This Linked Mission explores how to manage a
vineyard. The three support missions below
are run to support any Linked Mission,
but will help this mission.

This Linked Mission explores training
in general, but will be of use to the main Linked
Mission shown on the left.

This Linked Mission explores the enterprise
in general, but will be of use to the main Linked
Mission shown on the left.

This Linked Mission explores risk
in general, but will be of use to the main Linked
Mission shown on the left.

Diagram showing three Support Linked Missions *(only the Upkeep parts are shown)* used to
support a standard Linked Mission to resolve the management of a vineyard.

Some new roles in *Change-mapping*
Running large and complex missions more effectively

©CGI Joseph Chittenden

A real world example

*A baked bean manufacturer uses Change-mapping to record how 10,000 cans are produced. The 10,000 cans are sent to a warehouse which acts as a type of physical library. In addition data about **how** the cans were produced is sent to a data library. Although the different libraries are in different locations they still act as one Library.*

The roles shown on the diagram (see right) could be filled by one person or many depending on circumstances. For example security for physical information might be concerned with health and safety or asset management, while security for data might be who has clearance to view the data.

An overview

Back in Book 1 *(page 12)* we introduced a set of roles to help run basic Missions. But when you run large and complex missions, you may well need some more specialised roles to help things run smoothly. Most of these new roles are connected to how information is stored and shared.

Some new roles in Change-mapping

Security *(see Library, page 64)*
This role manages how information *(in any form)* gets **in** and **out** of the Library, and also other types of security, for example asset management of buildings.

Librarian *(see Library, page 64)*
This role manages how information is saved, categorised, and updated.

Archivist *(see Library, page 64)*
This role manages how information is archived, deleted, recreated and migrated.

Coordinator *(see Library, page 64)*
This role manages how information is delivered to the right people, in the right place at the right time.

Architect
This role manages how information is interpreted, especially looking at patterns of information. This will involve looking at the big picture and being able to dive into the details of specific missions *(with the help of the Library)*.
They will have a particular interest in the enterprise as a whole *(see page 56)*. For example, taking the image above, one mission would focus on one building, while the architect would want an overview of the entire city. and how things connect

This Linked Mission is exploring how to update a legal firm's ERP.

Pathfinder, Observer and Explorers

These roles (see Book 1, page 12) are used throughout the Linked Mission. In one particular session they want to explore uncertainties and use the SCAN tool (see Book 2, page 82). They fill-in the tool-sheet, keep a record for themselves and send a copy to the main Library.

Archivist

This new role is used once a Linked Mission is complete. Dealing with long term storage, deletion and so on.

Security   Librarian

These new roles deal with the information (in this example a SCAN tool-sheet) getting INTO the Library. Security makes sure the info can't hurt the Library and the Librarian categorises and stores the information.

Library

Another Linked Mission is exploring how to facilitate a merger.

Info request

Pathfinder, Observer and Explorers

These roles are used in this mission. They request any information about uncertainties from the Library. Once their request is approved, the SCAN tool-sheet is sent from the Library.

Security   Coordinator

These new roles deal with the information (in this example a SCAN tool-sheet) getting OUT of the Library. Security makes sure the info is allowed to leave the Library; the Coordinator makes sure who requested it will get it when needed.

A diagram showing how one piece of information *(in this example a SCAN tool-sheet)* could be stored and shared using the new roles such as a Librarian.

What are Learning deliverables?
Recording a process to support learning

CGI Joseph Chittenden

Capturing Learning deliverables

Any process from running an interview to building a ship can be recorded in multiple ways. One of the key methods of recording a process is to remember to record the process! Often when time is an issue, the process recording is removed. Possibly the best way to record a process is via video as you will be able to watch experts and see timings and why they are doing certain things. Arguably writing down the process without diagrams is the worst method as so much can be open to interpretation and guesswork.

Learning deliverables

Learning deliverables are mentioned throughout this book as items which can help others *(and you in the future)* recreate what you *(or others)* did.

Typically when someone is trying to resolve the issue, they won't have time to record how they resolved it.

This might not matter always but it could if someone else needed to recreate or re-engineer what you did five years later, for example. It is also useful to note when you had to move away from the planned course of action.

If we imagine that *Change-mapping* was used to plan how prototype binoculars *(such as the ones shown above)* were constructed. But as the binoculars were built no one recorded *how* they were built. Not recording how the binoculars were built has at least two disadvantages:

One, what if you want to build another set of binoculars using the same methods. Two, what if thirty years in the future somebody needs to disassemble the binoculars, knowing how it was built will help with its disassembly.

One advantage of recording how you perform any process, is the ability to replay it and improve it. This approach has been used in sport for many years, but why not use it for improving interview techniques or manufacturing furniture?

Learning deliverables can also help with running **Upkeep** missions *(see page 68)*. They are used to maintain a service or product, so having a record of how the service or product was built can be used in the future.

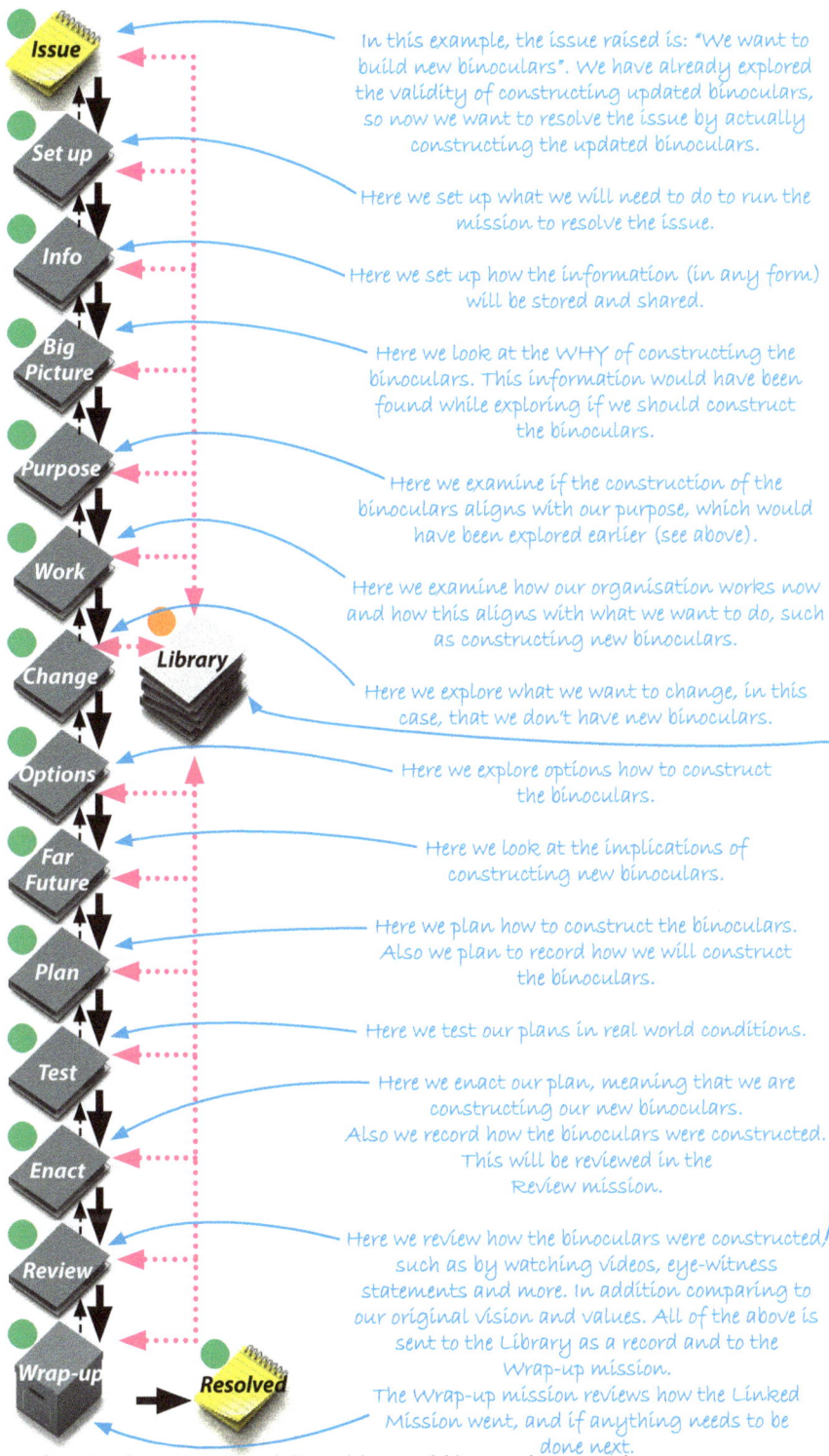

Issue — In this example, the issue raised is: "We want to build new binoculars". We have already explored the validity of constructing updated binoculars, so now we want to resolve the issue by actually constructing the updated binoculars.

Set up — Here we set up what we will need to do to run the mission to resolve the issue.

Info — Here we set up how the information (in any form) will be stored and shared.

Big Picture — Here we look at the WHY of constructing the binoculars. This information would have been found while exploring if we should construct the binoculars.

Purpose — Here we examine if the construction of the binoculars aligns with our purpose, which would have been explored earlier (see above).

Work — Here we examine how our organisation works now and how this aligns with what we want to do, such as constructing new binoculars.

Library / Change — Here we explore what we want to change, in this case, that we don't have new binoculars.

Options — Here we explore options how to construct the binoculars.

Far Future — Here we look at the implications of constructing new binoculars.

Plan — Here we plan how to construct the binoculars. Also we plan to record how we will construct the binoculars.

Test — Here we test our plans in real world conditions.

Enact — Here we enact our plan, meaning that we are constructing our new binoculars. Also we record how the binoculars were constructed. This will be reviewed in the Review mission.

Review — Here we review how the binoculars were constructed, such as by watching videos, eye-witness statements and more. In addition comparing to our original vision and values. All of the above is sent to the Library as a record and to the Wrap-up mission.

Wrap-up / Resolved — The Wrap-up mission reviews how the Linked Mission went, and if anything needs to be done next.

Diagram showing how Learning deliverables could be used to record a process

Adding context to an agile project
Using *Change-mapping* with project management software

Photograph source: Flickr, Mike McBey. CGI Train Joseph Chittenden

In brief
This part of the book was inspired by a question raised on the Tetradian Patreon page (www.patreon.com/tetradian) which explores Change-mapping and Whole-Enterprise Architecture. There, a question was raised about how to connect the context with using an IT software development program. Here we show how, using Change-mapping, the context can be explored and how it relates to every part of the project from top to bottom.

An overview
A software developer is running project management software and wants to understand more about the context surrounding the project. They decide to use *Change-mapping* to better understand what is valued and more within the project. Many project management programs work well with planning but fail to set the project in context, which can have huge ramifications as the project progresses. Here we look at how you could use *Change-mapping* in such a project.

Initiatives, epics and stories
Agile projects are often split into **initiatives** (a set of epics that have a common goal), **epics** (large sets of stories) and **stories** (stories are descriptions of user requirements). If we imagine that a software developer is developing software for a train sensor, the *initiative* is to have working software so that the sensor will function as intended. The *epics* include points such as making sure the wifi link talks to the main processor. One of the *stories* for that epic is that the sensor can't relay data if it can't communicate its data from the processor to the wifi.

Change-mapping and initiatives
Change-mapping can be used in various ways such as looking at the big picture of the *initiative*. With everyone trying their best to do their own part, sometimes the grasp on the big picture can be lost. Understanding the big picture can have large benefits when you get down to the details.
Here we will look at some of the parts of a Linked mission that can be used to explore the big picture of an *initiative*.

Who are the stakeholders?

The *stories* within the *initiative* describe the user's requirements, but it can be useful to understand the requirements of stakeholders who don't directly interact with a product or service, but can affect or be affected by it. In our train sensor example, we can concentrate on the software helping the people using it, but then fail to consider people who will train people how to use the sensor. We can use the **Holomap tool** (Book 2, page 22) to map out who are the stakeholders within our initiative. The Holomap tool can also be used to find what each stakeholder requires. For example what standards do your suppliers use? What do your clients value? The tools mentioned below can be used with the Holomap tool to know who to find more about.

Sense-making

What is the big-picture of the *initiative*? How does it fit into the software developer's story? Of course most organisations will know why they are working on a project, but not always... We can use the **Sense-making tool** (Book 2, page 10) to have a clear understanding of what you are trying to achieve and why. In our train sensor example, they failed to do this and as the project progressed *scope creep* started to cause issues, With some wanting the train sensor to have features that didn't match the overall story, for example making it too large which would make it too difficult to transport.

Standards, regulations and laws

What are the standards for the *initiative*? This again seems something that everyone would obviously know, but not always. Assumptions can have far reaching implications as the project progresses. For example, our train sensor was designed with the software using Fahrenheit to measure temperature, but nobody realised that the sensor was calibrated in Celsius. We can explore what standards and so on are required using the **Basic Context tool** (Book 1, page 68).

Being more effective

When we are deciding how we want our *initiative* to work, we need to make sure that what we do will effectively resolve our issue. If we reduce waste in one department but create more in another then we are not effective across the whole organisation and *initiative*. The **Effectiveness tool** (Book 2, page 34) explores effectiveness criteria which can be used from the enterprise level down to the smallest details.

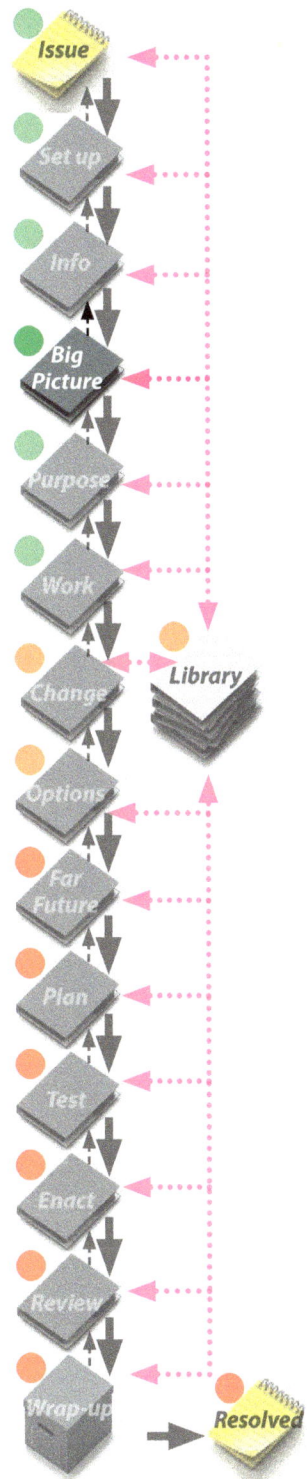

Some considerations for user requirements of a service or product such as software:
- *The user's gender*
- *The user's age*
- *Design for all*
- *Intuitive design*
- *The user's occupation*
- *Is the product or service used inside or outside?*
- *The country that the service or product is used in*
- *What are the conventions and customs used in that country?*
- *Is the product or service used day or night?*

Some potential locations the product or service could be used in
- *Home*
- *Office*
- *Road transport*
- *Factory*
- *Supermarket*
- *Entertainment venue*
- *City*
- *Motorway*
- *Airport*
- *Ship*
- *Aircraft*
- *Railway*
- *Farm*

What is valued within the initiative?

A software developer will have a set of values, while the end user may have a whole different set of values. Some may align and some may not. We can use the Holomap tool, mentioned earlier, with the **Value tool** *(Book 2, page 6)* to explore what each stakeholder values. A lot of values would seem obvious, but one person's obvious is not always another person's. For example a software developer may not know that the user values ease of use in the software over processor speed. The Value tool can be used here to split the *initiative* into four parts for each stakeholder. How does the client value aspects such as information? How much information do they need? It depends. How much information is required is explored in *(Book 1, page 56)*.

Initiatives and the enterprise

Agile projects have many advantages but can start to wander off into *scope creep* and *analysis-paralysis*. Also an *initiative* can sometimes align with your organisation's purpose but not with the overall enterprise or story. For example extracting more gold would be one type of *initiative*, but if that extraction ruined the local environment then the overall enterprise would be at risk. The **Guide tool** *(Book 2, page 26)* explores what must stay the same and what can change within an enterprise. Any *initiative* has the potential to change an enterprise, so knowing what can or cannot change can potentially save time and money down the line.

The service cycle

Knowing how a product or service will be used in real conditions, rather than ideal conditions, can greatly shape an *initiative* later on. Shown on the left are a few points to consider, for example when designing software.

These are part of the *initiative's* stories. Most will consider end users but with the Holomap tool and Value tools we can see how other stakeholders might be affected by your customers using a product or service. For example, a highly efficient airport with the latest IT systems, which is loved by shareholders and hated by locals because of flights arriving in the middle of the night. Another tool which can help to better understand *initiatives*, *epics* and *stories* is the **Service cycle tool** *(Book 2, page 30)*. With this tool we can see how a product or service is used at various stages.

Force majeure

So far we have looked at who the stakeholders are and what they require from the *initiative*. This can suggest that once we know this, then the *initiative* will work as intended. Most of the time this is true, but sometimes there are players within the *initiative* that can change everything in one fell swoop such as politics and forces of nature.

PEST

As we all have seen political forces can change the *initiative* overnight, the same applies to economic, social and technological forces which can sometimes change everything. When we connect this information with the other information found in tools such as Holomap, we can start to see trends and react to them.

Natural forces

We could design the best software for our train sensor, but it wouldn't matter if the sensor couldn't work in certain conditions. Dust for example, can ground the most sophisticated helicopters. Rats can chew through router cables disabling a multi-national investment firm. The **Knock-on effects tool** (Book 2, page 68) explores some factors which can blow an *initiative* out of the water. Risk is also explored further on page 104. In addition a few suggestions are shown on the right that ask where a product or service might be used.

Bringing it all together

We can see how with this information we can create a picture of the context in which our *initiative* sits. Finding this information is done just like any other *Change-mapping* mission or linked mission, by exploring, resolving or addressing an issue with small connected teams.

This information also acts like a checklist, to make sure that at least *most* of the important questions actually have been asked by *somebody*.

This information can then be referred to when making decisions about the details of a project such as developing software. If down the line the software code is about to be written for Fahrenheit, a quick check can confirm that before it had been specified that Celsius was the required measurement system. These fundamental questions can be so simple that it is assumed that somebody asked them.

But if nobody asks them, then we can rush to plan the wrong thing. Then no matter how clever the solution, it is still the wrong one.

Some factors which can affect a service or product such as software:
- *Weather, extreme heat*
- *Weather, extreme cold*
- *Weather, storms*
- *Weather, floods*
- *Wild-fires*
- *Dust*
- *Water*
- *Sand*
- *Insects/Vermin*
- *EM Interference*
- *UV*
- *High Pressure • Low Pressure*

Some potential natural environments the product or service could be used in
- *Mountains*
- *Desert*
- *Forest*
- *Ocean*
- *Marshland*
- *Floodplains*

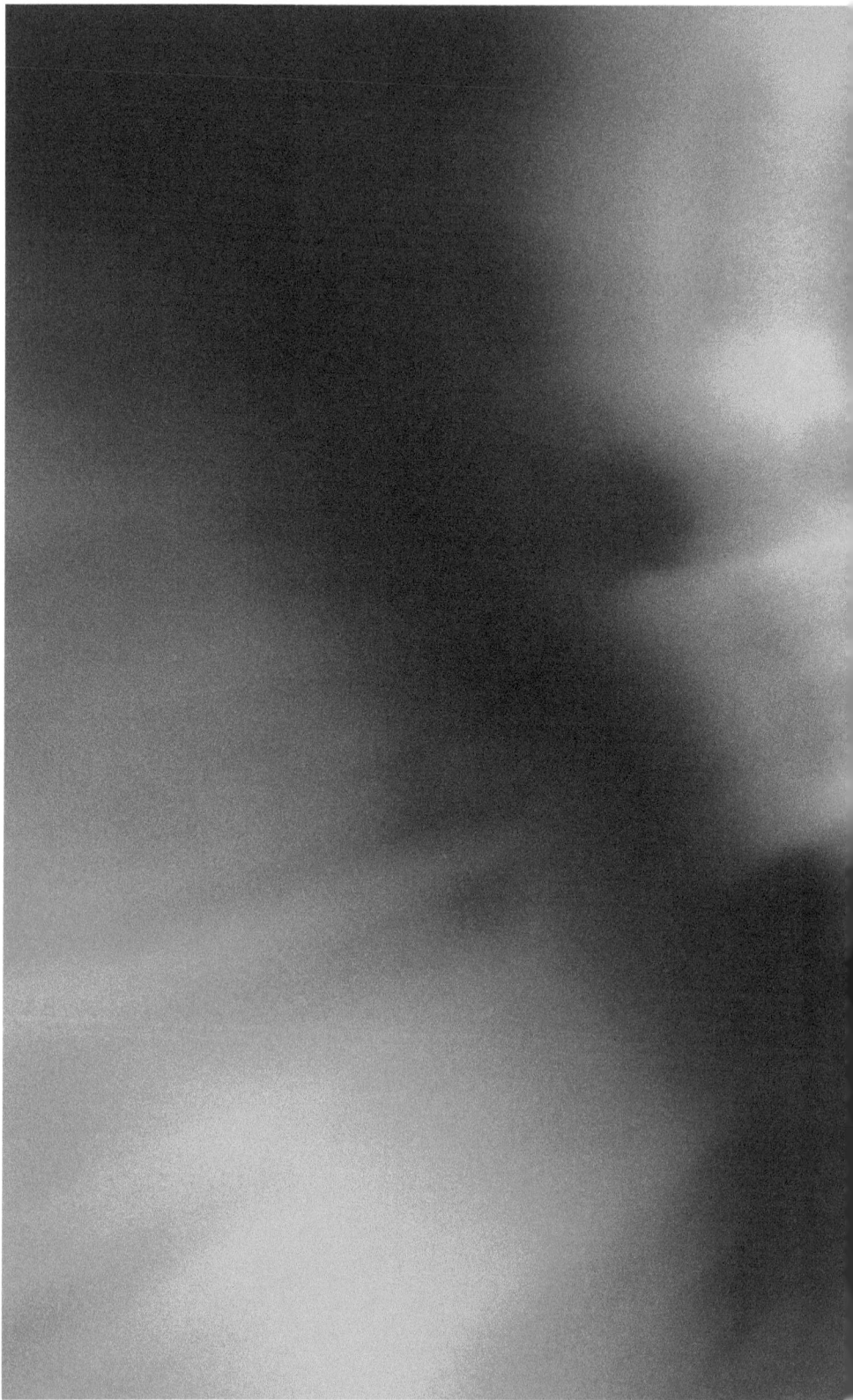

Part 3:
How to ask the
right questions

In the quest to find the answers to questions, are we
asking the right questions?
In this part of the book we present
a set of workshops. Each workshop poses a question
about your organisation and the enterprise
you are part of.

A set of questions to start discussions
Understanding *Whole Enterprise Architecture*

In brief
This part of the book discusses some key large-scale and far-reaching issues which can affect any organisation. Each discussion can be the focus of a Change-mapping mission to either learn Change-mapping or can be useful to explore these issues to make your organisation be more effective.

Exploring the *'why'* of an issue

The most likely reason you would use a system such as *Change-mapping* is to find the answer to something. Sometimes you may call in an expert to help find that answer, and of course this can be highly effective, but not always. It is similar to the old adage:

Give a man a fish and you feed him for a day, teach a man to fish and you feed him for life.

The problem with bringing in experts to give the right answers is twofold. Firstly they will often have a *one size fits all* answer and secondly you can become reliant on them rather than self-reliant.

A different approach is to learn how to ask the right questions, such as shown with *Change-mapping*.

In this part of the book we present a set of **questions**. These questions are taken from Tom Graves' well respected **Tetradian weblog**: *http://weblog.tetradian.com/*
There he regularly discusses subjects such Whole Enterprise Architecture, Business Architecture and more.
A small selection of posts from the Tetradian weblog are included in this part of the book which aim to act as catalysts for discussions about exploring the enterprise your organisation is part of. These discussions can be answered using *Change-mapping*, how this can be done is shown on the right.

How to use this part of the book

Each article in this section poses a question. Each question has profound implications for an organisation and how it sits within the enterprise it is part of.

These questions can be addressed using *Change-mapping* as described on **page iv**. What is found can be used to inform how your organisation can be more effective for any context.

Key

1 *Scenario*
A real world example of the issue raised by the article's question.

2 *Weblog reference*
The web address for the Tetradian weblog post on which the article is based.

3 *Article*
The main article which poses a question about Whole Enterprise Architecture. Most of the articles are spread over four pages.

4 *Change-mapping tool*
Change-mapping tools which can be used to answer specific parts of the article.

What is an enterprise?

It's about the story

Photograph source: Flickr, Mike McBey. CGI Train, Joseph Chittenden

The scenario

A Spanish railway operator has invested in a new fleet of high speed trains and feel that their organisation 'is' the enterprise. Most agreed until someone reminded them that they can't be the entire enterprise as they didn't own the railway lines on which their trains run. As this fact sunk in they realised that they also didn't 'own' their passengers either, who could quite easily change the overall story (or enterprise) by driving across Spain rather than using the trains. They decided that they needed to better understand what an enterprise actually was...

What is an enterprise? is based on the Tetradian weblog post: http://weblog.tetradian. com/2010/01/26/the-enterprise-is-the-story/

Every enterprise has a story, many of them, in fact

Yet there's also a deeper story that defines the enterprise itself, what the enterprise *is*. It's not just that the enterprise has a story: the enterprise *is* a story.

What's special about the enterprise-story is that every participant in the enterprise chooses to engage with that story. So how could and should that story be told, by whom, in what forms, via what means or media? And since it's a story that's also shared by every participant in the enterprise, there are some real questions about ownership here: if the enterprise is a story, who really owns the enterprise?

The organisation and the enterprise

A common misconception is that the enterprise *is* the organisation, that *the business* and *the enterprise* are one and the same. But whilst it's true that an organisation is a specific type of enterprise, the enterprise is rarely an organisation as such, because the two terms are fundamentally different:
• *An organisation is bounded by rules.*
• *An enterprise is bounded by shared commitment.*

he enterprise is always much larger than the organisation, because it provides a unifying theme for everyone within the organisation, all of the organisation's partners and suppliers, and all of the organisation's clients and prospects and hence helps to define the *space* in which marketing and the like may take place. Crucially, this theme is also the key reference-point for all those who interact with the organisation in other ways, such as government, or non-clients in the broader community, who are still *stakeholders* in what the organisation is and does, even if they play little or no active part in it. The organisation's *anti-clients (those who, for any reason, actively dislike or distrust the organisation)* will often question or challenge the organisation's purported role and relationship to the enterprise.

The Holomap tool (Book 2, page 22) can be used to map out who are the stakeholders across an enterprise.

The organisation itself chooses a specific role within that broader enterprise, a choice that opens a space for others to take up other roles in the same story. This difference in roles is what enables interactions between the players, within the terms of the various intersecting economies of the enterprise, such as transactions, attention and trust. If the organisation presents itself as *the enterprise*, it leaves no space for others to engage in the organisation's enterprise and no reason to do so, either. So this distinction between *organisation* and *enterprise* is no academic quibble, but utterly fundamental to any understanding of the relationship between the organisation and its surrounding ecosystem.

It becomes useful, essential, even, to ask who or what it is that sends us on that mission to address the enterprise. At the enterprise level, the key to this is the enterprise vision, the single unifying theme that provides a common aim for all participants in the enterprise. The vision and accompanying values form the basis for any number of stories that express that vision. Almost by definition, there will be at least as many stories as there are people engaged in the enterprise, all of them different, because each person has a slightly viewpoint into the vision, but they will all also be identifiably about the *same* vision, or some aspect of the same vision.

The Visioning tool (Book 2, page 14) can be used to explore stakeholder's vision for an enterprise.

Possessing the story

The enterprise-story is where people connect with the enterprise. It's also how they connect with the enterprise. Each person in the enterprise commits to and participates in the enterprise-story, in their own unique way, if only as a side-effect of engagement in the enterprise and its story. This is what makes marketing possible: marketers create a story that in some way relates to the story of the overall enterprise, to open the way for a connection with the organisation.

Who owns the story?

In the past there's been a simple answer to that question: the organisation owns the story. Possesses the story, more precisely. The story as trademark, as brand, as private property. The story told only as a one-way broadcast from the marketing department, the PR department, through channels that the organisation also exclusively controls and owns. The marketplace itself has changed from a public space, to a controlled, filtered, private property. And if the organisation seems to own the story, it's easy to believe that the organisation *is* the enterprise.

People also don't respond well to command and coercion: they retreat back to their own story, offering only the absolute minimum of commitment needed to get by. Hence the more an organisation tries to control the story, the more it prevents engagement in its own enterprise. Under those circumstances, clients easily become anti-clients with serious yet seemingly-unexpected impacts on the organisation. The only way forward is for the organisation to loosen its grip on the enterprise, in other words, to let go of its increasingly desperate attempts to command and control.

Losing control of the story

Not that the organisation has much choice now about relinquishing that control. It's no longer one-to-many, but many-to-many.

Social media also enables many-to-one messages, so that the organisation can sometimes even find its own voice swamped and silenced. An organisation's anti-clients can also now wield every bit as much influence as the organisation itself: a viral campaign can destroy many years' worth of carefully-crafted corporate messages in a matter of minutes.

What makes letting-go hard is the *'need'* to possess the *'true version'* of the story. Others' complaints about our organisation may seem *'unfair'*, for example – yet they are a real part of that story, and each provides its own thread to create a richer fabric of story. Yet a random collection of themes and views is not a story: so how do we ensure that the threads do hold together into a unified, unifying vision for the enterprise?

Learning from the storytellers

One useful source of guidance here is the storytellers themselves, particularly the creators of film and books. People engage in these stories, intensely: the term *fan* is shorthand for *fanatic*, and with good reason.

The exact same applies to the story for a business-enterprise: without shared-commitment to the enterprise-story, the business fades and is forgotten. Marketers aim to do the same, by likewise creating a story and brand-champions from celebrities who encompass the spirit of the story.

The challenge is to ensure that the story allows this openness but still retains its integrity. Storytellers do this by viewing themselves not as *possessors* of the story, but as its custodians: the difference is subtle, but extremely important.
Another reason why you need to understand transmedia* in relation to the enterprise-story is that it's through the *many-to-many* social-media that your anti-clients are most likely to communicate with each other and with the wider community, and where *anti-stories* about your enterprise will develop and spread. If you don't keep track of what's happening in that world, your own *anti-stories* will seem to arrive out of nowhere – catching you off-guard with nowhere to go. So these media give you a place to engage with those stories at the earliest possible opportunity – and help bring them back to align with the overall enterprise-story.

Yet there's another important catch here too: the more overtly you align with the enterprise-story and its underlying vision and values, the greater engagement you can gain from your stakeholders; but those other stakeholders will also hold you more accountable to that story, too. Playing fast-and-loose with the story, or trying to rig it solely to your advantage over others, will be a very dangerous mistake: in the new internet age of immersive transparency, any perceived betrayal of the enterprise-story by the purported custodians of that story is probably the quickest way of all to create vast numbers of anti-clients, which can kill your company stone-dead in days if you're not very careful indeed. Responsibility matters here, especially your responsibilities to, with and for the enterprise-story.

The enterprise is a story. But the organisation is not the whole of the enterprise: it never was. And the organisation does not possess the story: it never did.

*Transmedia is the technique of telling a single story or story experience across multiple platforms and formats using current digital technologies. *Wikipeida*

The Sense-making tool
(Book 2, page 10) can be used to better understand an issue which the enterprise aims to resolve or address.

In our rail example, the rail operator explored its place inside the overall enterprise of people travelling across Spain. They saw beyond physical assets such as trains, that there were other assets, such as trust. Keeping customers aware of delays, rather than never admitting to delays, allowed the customers to trust the operator. Engaging with customers on social media helped 'humanise' the operator.

What are the perils of single focus?
Learning to avoid bias

Photograph source: Flickr, Prince Roy. CGI Truck from Turbosquid

The scenario

A logistics company faced rising fuel costs and increased customer expectations. Other areas such as recruiting and training new drivers was seen as unimportant. But as their drivers started to 'age-out' suddenly a panic ensued about where to find new trained drivers. Other more far-sighted competitors had a wider focus allowing them to adapt to ever changing circumstances. They also regularly placed heads of departments in different departments, so that they could better understand each others' priorities and needs.

What are the perils of single focus? is based on the Tetradian weblog post: http://weblog.tetradian. com/2015/05/06/rbpea- dangers-of-anything- centrism/

* Some may be unfamiliar with architecture in a business context. An architecture within an organisation is: the components, those component's capabilities and how they interact. For example one component might be logistics and delivers parcels and that it interacts with the HR department.

An architecture* may have a centre

In fact most types of architecture work best if there's a central focus.

Yet the process of creating an architecture must not have a single focus.

We need to explore how careless or premature framing of a context can itself impose artificial constraints on how we see or understand an architecture. Mis-framing the real context can make it almost impossible to develop a viable architecture for that context.

In reality, every real-world context has many, many interweaving threads and themes, but for this purpose, let's simplify it right down to a straightforward interaction between just two departments: Logistics and HR.

Note that the relationship between the departments is dynamic, like a ball rolling along the road. Sometimes one department is more prominent, then the other, changing all the time, and depending also on which way we see them.

Note that the relationship between the departments is balanced – sometimes one department is more prominent, then the other, but there is an overall balance between them.

Note that the relationship between the departments is fractal, each department contains within itself elements of the other, potentially onward to infinity.

Note that the relationship between the departments forms *a system* – dynamic, balanced, fractal, each element interdependent on the others, each element an *equal citizen* with all of the others.

Yet note how easy it is to pick on one element as *the centre* of the system, and downgrade or even ignore the importance of others. For example:
A selective snapshot of a dynamic system will typically emphasise one element. If we then fall into the *policy-based evidence* trap, Gooch's Paradox, that *things not only have to be seen to be believed, but also have to be believed to be seen.* Then subsequent snapshots will tend to be taken at points which re-emphasise the apparent *priority* of that one theme.

Some fall for the *statistics trap*: failing to understand that *high-probability* does not mean *will always happen*, or that *low-probability* does not mean *will never happen*.

Some have a personal preference for one department, or a personal dislike towards another department.

Some fail to understand the inherent fractal nature of most real-world systems, that each element also contains every other element, and so try to force-fit every element into simplistic categories.

These cognitive-bias errors *(and many others like them)* may be combined, of course. The end-result, though, is that the context is mis-framed: one department becomes viewed as *The Centre*, around which all others must revolve.
In many cases, attention is withdrawn so much from those departments that are not *The Centre* that they fade away from visibility, becoming *hidden in plain sight*.
When that happens, not only does the system cease to be dynamic, but every discussion is dragged back to that one *Centre*. The result is that, to make the system work again as a viable system, we all but have to use a crowbar to get any attention paid to any other of the departments within that organisation. Yet because of the need for such overt action,

The Notes tool *(Book 2, page 64)* uses the metaphor of a film to explore the different departments within an organisation.

we'll risk immediately being accused of being *against* the chosen *Centre*.

Practical implications for an organisation

Within an organisation, every department will usually attempt to be or become *The Centre* around which the architecture supposedly *must* revolve. We need to become fierce defenders of overall balance.

BDAT[2] *(Business, Data, Applications, Technology)* pushes us to interpret everything within the organisation in terms of its impact on *Big-IT*. Increasingly, though, we're also starting to see an equivalent over-emphasis on a view of *business-architecture* still over-focussed on IT, yet ultimately based on an unacknowledged assumption that the only possible measure of value is money. If we try to tackle this from above the department, there will be too much resistance. A more effective approach is to tackle this issue on the ground and establish a beachhead to implement change.

How to avoid a single focus

Some straightforward tactics that you can use to tackle a single focus include:

– What would the department look like if we moved the viewpoint all the way above this department, and then came back down in a different department? *(such as for user-experience elements in app-architectures, where we must focus on people first).*

– What would the system look like if *The Centre* wasn't there at all? *(such as where existing IT becomes unavailable in a disaster-recovery context).*

– How might someone from a different department run your department and you run theirs *(constructively!)*. A fresh perspective can make one appreciate the struggles others face. The old adage *"Walk a mile in a man's shoes, before criticising him"* for example.

In a business-architecture context, viewing the organisation as *The Centre Of Everything* is so endemic that it's all but essential to do at least some assessment of what would happen in the broader shared-enterprise if the organisation was not there. This is a blunt but often effective way to break a habit of incipient organisation over-focus. It's only if we do this that we start to gain some understanding of what the organisation actually does bring to the shared-enterprise table, and so the real basis for its business-models and suchlike. Viewed

2. BDAT is a way of presenting an organisation's IT requirements, but it can be seen as biased towards IT.

Business Architecture	
Data Architecture	App. Architecture
Technology Architecture	

outside-in as much as *inside-out*, in systematic modelling that maintains the overall balance throughout.

The catch, of course, is that defence of *over focus on one department* is rarely rational, and the attacks on anyone who challenges the purported absolute-centrality of that chosen theme, even inadvertently, can be unpleasant, to say the least. One approach is to keep the focus on the big-picture, the broader-context, with a strong emphasis on what we're *for* rather than what we're *against*.

Also remember that, however much of a nuisance it may be, that arbitrarily-chosen *Centre* is still a valid part of the organisation, that is another reminder that we do need to pay attention to that department too at times, despite the very real need to keep pulling attention back to all the other departments as well.

Tackling *singular focus* is tough – probably some of the hardest and most challenging work that people in business ever have to do. But we really dare not avoid that work, because if any form of *singular focus* is allowed to take hold, the architecture will fail.

The Inside/Out tool
(Book 2, page 6) can be used to explore how an organisation functions.

In our logistics example, the company found that they had focused on one specific department, with everything revolving around the drivers. They found the time to make department heads sit down and openly state their wants and needs. HR which had been marginalised, felt that training needed to have a higher importance.
This open exchange led to seasoned drivers helping train and recruit new drivers.

Further reading

Four principles for a sane society: Summary
How do we make sense of the big-picture in enterprise-architecture? The really big-picture? Read more at:
ttp://weblog.tetradian.com/2013/02/20/four-principles-summary/

On power
What is power? Where does it come from? Where does it go? Who has it? Who doesn't have it? Who should have it? Who shouldn't have it? And why? – or why not, for that matter – to any of those questions…? Read more at:
ttp://weblog.tetradian.com/2019/11/01/on-power/

What do you need for a viable business architecture?

Making sense when planning a business

Photograph source: CGTextures. CGI Drone, Joseph Chittenden

The scenario

A UAV (unmanned aerial vehicle) manufacturer wanted to better understand why certain projects were completed on time, while others were plagued by delays. They started to examine their business architecture to reveal what was happening across the entire organisation. This examination involved starting at the enterprise level and gradually working down into the fine details of specific tasks such as inventory storage and marketing.

What do we need for a viable business architecture? is based on the Tetradian weblog post: http://weblog.tetradian. com/2020/01/03/building-blocks-for-viable-bizarch/

What's the purpose of business-architecture?

The role of business-architecture is to build and maintain a clear picture of the structures and stories that the organisation will need, in order to do its business. Or, in short, to maintain the architecture of *the business of the business* in context of the organisation's markets and the respective broader shared-enterprises, and then help others use that picture to guide the implementation of that organisation's structures, services and operations, from a business perspective.

In functional terms, business-architecture sits as a bridge between strategy, product- and/or service-design, organisation-design, marketing and change-management, and also some aspects of operations-design and knowledge-management.

The services that business-architecture would provide relate mainly to guidance for and arbitration between each of those organisational-functions above *(strategy, product-design etc)* for which it acts as a bridge, in relation to any questions about *the business of the business* as a unified whole.

The key effect of the absence of a distinct business-architecture is that business-analysts and others would be forced to make often arbitrary guesses about what *the business of the business* actually is. Such guesses are rarely consistent with each other, are often too easily influenced by vendors' *solutioneering*, and may well be just plain wrong.

What capacity for business-architecture will an organisation need?

It's probable that the only honest answer would be *It depends…* The most common key factor here is organisational size and complexity. As the business grows in scale and complexity, the need for a dedicated business-architecture role, and, later, a dedicated team, will likewise increase. Probably the closest parallel would be the organisation's business-strategy function: a business-architecture team is likely to need to be roughly the same size as the strategy-team, though unlike strategists, business-architects are more likely to be a distributed-team working more directly with and between other business-functions.

What maturity will an organisation need before it can gain real value from business-architecture?

We could argue that the correct answer is *any maturity at all*. For example, one of the times we most need a business-architecture is right at the start, when we technically have no organisational-maturity at all. What differs at different levels of maturity is the emphases and priorities for the types of activities we need to undertake, and we can use an explicit maturity-model to guide us in this.

What must a company have in place to support a successful and useful business-architecture?

If we presume that what's meant by *have* is the set of artefacts, documents, diagrams, models and suchlike, that will be used to guide conversations on business-architecture and its use, dependent on the architecture purpose, capacity and maturity as above.

For the absolute top-level for the business-architecture, the single most important part of this top-level is the *enterprise-vision*. This a very brief summary, often no more than half a dozen words, about the *what*, *how* and *why* that holds the entire enterprise together. Here, the term *the enterprise* is not the same as *the organisation*: it relates to the shared-enterprise that the organisation serves, and within which the organisation does its business. This is much broader in scope,

The Visioning tool
(Book 2, page 14) can be used to explore stakeholder's vision for an enterprise.

The Value tool
(Book 2, page 6) can be used to explore what is valued within an enterprise

The Basic Context tools
(Book 1, page 68) can be used to explore, success criteria, standards and more.

The Inside/Out tool
(Book 2, page 6) can be used to explore how an organisation functions.

not just broader than the organisation or even its market, but a scope bounded by a shared-story that would always continue to exist even if the organisation and market did not. Values, success-criteria, standards, laws and regulations all devolve from that enterprise-vision, it's that important. The organisation then positions itself in relation to that enterprise, via its own mission and vision, which are necessarily subordinate to the enterprise-vision itself, and *not* the other way round.

The enterprise-vision provides the anchor for looking *outward* from the organisation, towards its customers, suppliers, investors and other partners. We then need to link to that outward enterprise by looking *inward* back into the organisation itself. Hence the other essential business-architecture artefact, to aid with this, is the capability-model *(sometimes known by other terms such as Functional Business Model)*. This model describes what the organisation does, in a deliberately abstract way, the capabilities or functions that are needed for the organisation to do its business.
At its simplest possible level *(Tier 1)*, almost every business-organisation would have a capability model that looks somewhat like this:

	Manage the business			
Contact customer	Accept orders	Process orders	Deliver orders	Fulfil orders
	Support the business			

At the next level of detail *(Tier 2)*, there's more differentiation, though organisations in the same industry would share a similar capability-model, to which industry-wide standards are often associated.

In business-architecture, we would typically develop our capability-model to at least *Tier-3*, a more organisation-specific level, at which point it becomes hugely useful to the organisation.

	Manage the business Such as managing equipment purchases seen as vital and cant be questioned?			
Contact customer uch as developing and maintaining advertising	**Accept orders** Such as accepting internet orders	**Process orders** Such as assemble all items for the order	**Deliver orders** Such as package and get ready for courier delivery	**Fulfil orders** Such as verify customer has received the
	Support the business Such as maintain warehouse Background stuff but not in main profit line			

Business architecture or "Business architecture"?

here's one important proviso related to all of the above: the oncept of business-architecture described above is not the ame as the so-called "business-architecture" in certain current nterprise-architecture frameworks.

1 both approaches, business-architecture is regarded as a omewhat specialist sub-domain of a broader *enterprise-rchitecture*. But that is almost the only similarity between he two approaches.

1 the approach described here: *Business-architecture* is terally *the architecture of the organisation's business*, in ontext of *enterprise-architecture* as a literal *the architecture f the enterprise*. The focus of attention in each architecture is lways **people-first**, not **technology-first**. Technologies may e important, but only ever as an enabler in context of the usiness and the enterprise itself.

lowever, in some *enterprise*-architecture frameworks, he emphasis is the other way round: 'technology-first, not eople-first. Technology concerns take priority over people oncerns and the effective definition of *enterprise-architecture*. 1 those frameworks it is not *the architecture of the enterprise*, ut actually *the architecture of enterprise-IT. (Or, rather, the rchitecture of the organisation's IT, since there is a strong endency to regard 'organisation' and 'enterprise' as the same hing).* Their effective concept of 'business-architecture' is best ummarised as *anything not-IT that might affect IT*, which night perhaps be valid if our sole interest is the IT, but is a lassic *cart-before-horse* misframing if our real concern is the rchitecture of the business itself.

In our UAV manufacturer example, it was found that technology was dictating how the business operated rather than the other way round. They broke their business down into the different tiers (shown left). This detailed examination revealed that certain departments were stock-piling certain parts, but had forgotten where the parts were stored. This meant other departments resorted to ordering the same parts which led to delays and increased costs. An overhaul of their ERP system removed this blockage and improved production.

Are you selling a service or a product?

How to differentiate your offer in a changing market

Photograph source: Wikipedia,Martin St-Amant
Cpl Binoculars, Jason Crittenden

The scenario

A surveying company had prided itself on making the best equipment on the market. But cheaper imports had meant that it was hard to compete. They had tried to reduce costs, but this had led to a loss of quality, which led to a loss of sales.

They re-examined what they actually offered to their customers and often their customers' customers. They wanted reliability over anything, even cost. The surveying equipment manufacturer instead decided to compete on quality and service over low prices. This commitment to quality led to customers trusting the brand and increasing sales.

Are we selling a product or a service? is based on the Tetradian weblog post: http://weblog.tetradian. com/2020/12/11/service- product-service-promise- and-product/

A promise of future value

In sales, the only thing actually sold is a promise of future value.

Services take action towards that promise.

Products are the outcomes of that action and/or records or confirmations of what we did towards that promise.

Service and *product* are not fundamentally different, but instead are just different types of views into a continual flow of creation and change of value. What we see as *service* is a set of activities where value is being changed; what we see as *product* is a static snapshot of value at a particular moment or specific set of conditions. A product exists only in a gap between services; and the boundary of a service is where we choose to draw that boundary, so in turn we make products *visible* or *invisible* according to where we draw those boundaries. In that sense, services lead to products lead to services lead to products, and so on, potentially ad-infinitum.

Yet let's look at this from a sales-perspective. Whether we're nominally selling service or product, what we actually sell is a promise: we then have to deliver on that promise. In terms of the structure, that relationship would look something like this:

| Our Promise | ▶ | Our Service | ▶ | Our Product | ▶ |

Even if we're nominally selling a service, there should always be some kind of product at the end-point of that service-provision, to indicate that service has indeed been provided.

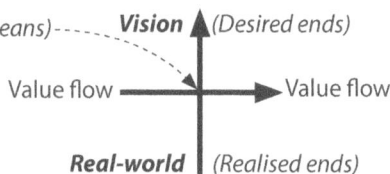

Service (means) - - - - - - **Vision** ▲ *(Desired ends)*

Value flow ◀———————————▶ Value flow

Real-world | *(Realised ends)*

Any service sits at an intersection between two different axes of value. The first is the *horizontal* flow of value – the supply-chain where each service adds a bit more value for the next one in the chain. The other axis is a *vertical* connection to what is commonly described as *values*. The shared-story or *enterprise* within which the service-provider positions itself. At a whole-of-business level, we would most commonly see this as the overall market, defining rules and standards so on to which each player within that market must align. Though the *enterprise* does actually extend beyond just the market, to the community, the country and more.

When we look more closely, each transaction between players in the supply-chain is made up of multiple interactions. Some of these occur before the main transaction, setting up the conditions for that transaction, the promise that will guide the detail of the transaction. Some of these interactions will occur during what we would see as *the transaction*. Some occur after the transaction, in effect verifying that the promise has been met.

A gap between services, is always and only bridged via some form of product. Which means that there will often be a lot of service-products moving back and forth across each gap, in addition to the one **Product** that everyone can see. When we explore the full extent of supply-chain or value-web, the sheer number of products, and different types of product, can soon seem overwhelming.

Yet we can reduce this down to something more manageable via a simple partitioning of the activities of a service, along two axes: *before, during, after*, and *inbound-oriented, internal ('this')*, and *outbound-oriented*.

We can give abstract labels to each of those partitions, though it's easy enough to find real-world labels for those partitions, for example from a manufacturing context.

Note, though, that that's only the interactions along that *horizontal*-axis of value-flow. For any real-world service, we would also need other interactions that connect across that *vertical* axis of values.

And every exchange or transaction across every gap between every pairing of services and child-services and subsidiary-services, always follows the same overall pattern. *(If it doesn't follow that pattern, it's likely to fail, especially in the longer term.)* The pattern is what we might term *the Service-Cycle*.

The Service Cycle

The Service cycle tool (Book 2, page 30) can be used to map out the stages of a service from the perspective of a customer and your organisation.

The Service Cycle is a more-detailed version of *before, during, after*: in particular, it tells us more about what needs to happen in the *before* and the *after*, and the typical sequence for what needs to happen.

In the *before* part, we establish the promise:

First, both parties verify shared-purpose and context, a connection via that *vertical-axis* of shared-values, as an anchor for the value-proposition. A value-proposition is a bridge between perceived-value *(horizontal-axis)* and the respective values of the players and the shared-enterprise as a whole *(vertical-axis)*. This will typically involve aspirational-assets such as reputation and brand.

Next, both parties verify who the parties are, and also verify the applicable scope. In a sales context, this would typically be person-to-person. This often involves relational-assets that represent and record the links between the respective actors. Next, both parties establish the agreement for action, the requirements to be addressed in the transaction, and the rules and standards and suchlike that should apply. This is the promise itself, a commitment typically expressed in forms such as a sales-contract. This will typically involve virtual-assets such as data-flows, signed contracts or paper-records.

At that point, we wait for some kind of trigger-event that shifts from *before* to *during*. The trigger may follow on immediately, such as the acceptance of the agreement by both parties; or else it might wait indefinitely for some external event, and may never actually be triggered at all, as in the case of insurance-agreement. Either way, when the event does occur, we begin to take action on the promise:

First, do any required actions to set up the required service. *(Note: in the terms used in this series, it's always a service – a product is an outcome of service, not the action itself.)* This step will be required if there's been a gap between promise and action – such as a gap of time, or location, or, in a classic business-to-business sales-context, where the person receiving any goods is different from the person who signed off on the purchase.

Next, run the service that will enact the transaction. *(Again, remember, it's always a service, because any activity always takes place within the context and boundaries of a service: any product to be delivered is an outcome of that service.)* Note also that there must be an identifiable end-condition for the service, such as a specific product returned.

Next, once the end-condition is met, complete the action, including verification of any products to be output from the service. This includes all action-records to be returned to the respective *interested parties*, within the organisation, or beyond *(such as to auditors)*.

At that point there's an implicit transition from *during* to *after*. This needs to trigger off a set of activities to verify compliance to the promise. The key purpose of these activities is to build and sustain trust, across the shared-enterprise as a whole, because if that trust is lost, so is the enterprise:

First, complete for the agreement. In a commercial context, we need to ensure that everything that we promised to do and/or deliver has been done. And for all respective stakeholders in that promise, not solely the respective *customer*. In return, we need to ensure that the customer *(and, again, each related stakeholder)* has delivered on their part of the agreement. *(Note that the service-cycle does not stop here: falling for the 'quick-profit cycle' mistake, and jumping straight back from here to the 'Conversation/contract' phase with a new prospect in a new service-cycle is a guaranteed way to cause failure in the longer-term).*

Next, complete for the relationship. The aim here is verify and sustain trust at a personal level, typically with the nominal client, but often with others as well.

Finally, complete for the shared-enterprise, the shared-story that anchors the vision and values for the shared-enterprise. The aim here is to verify trust at the transpersonal level *(the enterprise, the community, the country and more)*.
There also needs to be consistent effort to identify anti-client risks, both potential and actual anti-clients, and seek out any kurtosis risks* that could not just bring down a single organisation, but in some cases place an entire industry at risk.

In our surveying equipment example, the manufacturer had gained 'anti-clients' who were dissatisfied with how the brand was. In a bold move the manufacturer contacted some of those anti-clients and asked them what they felt needed to change. Many of the anti-clients became 'brand champions' as they saw how the brand was changing to quality over price. This led to increased trust in the brand with many on social media, unasked, endorsing the company's products.

*Kurtosis risk is discussed further on page 106.

How applicable are *best practices*?
Adapt, then adopt

Photograph source: Wikipedia, Asco.
CGI Dump truck, Joseph Chittenden

The scenario
A gold mining operation had followed 'best practice' diligently while working in Africa. This had worked effectively for them for years and so it seemed that 'best practice' would work for their new gold mine in South America. This presumption was to be sorely tested when they found that the road infrastructure was completely different, causing them to not even be able to transport the gold from the mines. They quickly learnt that unquestioningly following 'best practice' was not as effective as adapting 'best practice' and in time adopting new 'best practices'.

How applicable are best practices? is based on the Tetradian weblog post: http://weblog.tetradian. com/2012/12/19/best-practices-adapt-then-adopt/

Best practices – adapt, then adopt
Just how applicable are *best practices*? How certain can we be that they'll be *best* for each seemingly-equivalent context?

Best-practices are, in essence, methods that have worked well in one specific context. But that's the trap: its *bestness* is context-dependent, which means that it may not be *best* in another context. And if we focus only on the method, we have no way to work out whether it would or would not be best for our own specific context.
We will use the SCAN tool to illustrate this issue, as shown right *(For more detail about the Scan tool see Book 2, page 82)*. To make practical sense of this, we need to draw clear distinctions between methods, mechanics and approaches:

In unskilled work, it is not so much *best practice* as *right practice*: methods are more akin to *scientific law* and suchlike. Context does not count here: what the method does will always be the same, everywhere, and will always lead to the

Before →
the issue is
resolved

Complicated but controllable	**Ambiguous** but actionable

Planning →
how to
resolve the
issue

Simple and straightforward	**Not-known,** none of the above

How the issue
is being →
resolved

Certain → **Uncertain**

After the issue
is resolved

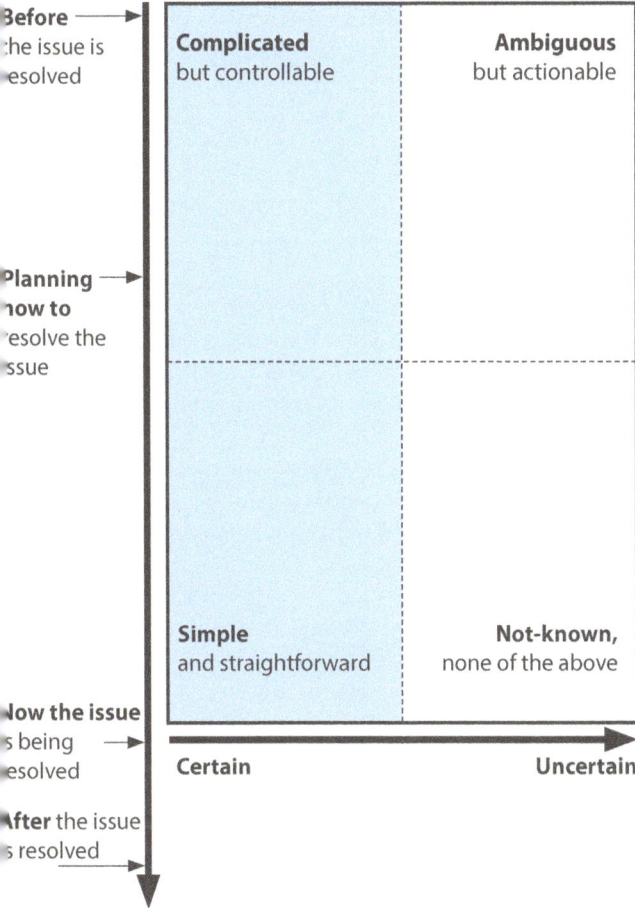

same results. Yet that will only work where everything does
remain the same, or where the supposedly-scientific *law* does
apply. In other words, over on the *certainty* side of the
SCAN tool[4].

By contrast, skilled-work must be able to tackle uncertainty,
the whole space indicated by the SCAN tool. Which means
that sometimes there's certainty, and sometimes there isn't;
and context most definitely can make a difference. That is why
we're forced here to think more in terms of *best-practice*,
a value-based view, rather than *right-practice*,
a *truth*-based view.

In effect, each method is a balance between the mechanics
and the approaches of the work-context:
The mechanics are *objective*, that which remains the same
everywhere, the content, the applicable *scientific laws* and
suchlike. The approaches are *subjective*, that which may be

different anywhere or everywhere, the context, the personal, locally-distinctive and unique.

What works well in one place, one person, one organisation, may not work well with another. How can we know what to use, and what not to use, where, when, how, and why?

In practice, we need to adapt each *best-practice* to our context, before we adopt it in our context.

Yet there's actually nothing in *best-practices* themselves that can tell us anything about this: they're just methods, someone-else's merging-together of the mechanics and the approaches for their specific context. To apply them to our context, we must:
– Separate out the context-independent mechanics from the original context-specific approaches.
– Identify, if possible, why these practices were *best* in that specific context.
– Identify the approaches that apply in our specific context(s).
– Re-combine the context-independent mechanics with the approaches for our context(s).
– Adapt further as required for each scale or sub-context.
– Adopt as context-specific method for the respective context or sub-context.
– Re-assess and review each method on a periodic basis to adapt to changing skills and changing contexts.
This applies to every purported *best-practice*. Which needs to be customised to the local context, adapted, before it can be adopted to work well in that context.

To do that separating-out of mechanics from approaches in the method, we need good analysis and assessment-skills, and it's often a lot harder than it looks.

See page iv for a description of an enterprise.

To identify what applies in our context, what work-arounds will be needed in our context, and so on, we're going to need a solid enterprise-architecture*, or at least a solid understanding of the respective domain-architectures** that apply in each context.

** A Domain architecture is a distinct part of the organisation which attempts to resolve or address a particular theme within the enterprise, such as the needs of the marketing department.

It is probably not possible to do this well without a proper enterprise-architecture, meaning a literal *architecture of the enterprise*, not merely the architecture of the business or the architecture of the enterprise-IT.

Adapt. Then adopt.

Further reading

Decision-making – linking intent and action [3]

How is it that what we actually do in the heat of the action can differ so much from the intentions and decisions we set beforehand? How can we bring them into better alignment, to 'keep to the plan'? And how does this affect our enterprise-architectures? Read more at:

http://weblog.tetradian.com/2012/01/08/decision-making-linking-intent-and-action-3/

There's no short-cut to experience

At least he was open about it, I guess. *"Tell you what I'll do"*, he says to my colleague here in Guatemala, *"I'll find you a client, then I'll sit in, learn everything you do, and then I'll apply it in my own business. How does that sound to you?"*

Uh, no. Not a good idea. Not just because it's a really bad deal from our perspective, but much more that Reality Department really doesn't work that way: there's no short-cut to experience. Read more at:

http://weblog.tetradian.com/2012/04/30/no-shortcut-to-experience/

Unbreaking

Current mainstream EA is broken, more broken and yet more broken, and has real problems with wickedness. But what can we do about this? How can we mend EA, make it unbroken? Read more at:

http://weblog.tetradian.com/2012/09/04/unbreaking/

Enterprise-architecture is wicked

How do we cope with the wickedness of EA?
What I mean here is the kind of *'wickedness'* that underpins wicked-problems – because as I understand enterprise-architecture, most of the issues we face in enterprise-architecture are wicked-problems. Read more at:

http://weblog.tetradian.com/2012/09/03/ea-is-wicked/

Methods, mechanics, approaches

Why doesn't 'best-practice' work as best-practice everywhere? And what is it that makes a skill a skill?

For me, this one goes way back to work I did for my Masters degree, nigh on forty years ago. And to me, the answer to both of those questions is the same: methods, mechanics, approaches. But we probably need to do a brief discursion in order to get there. Read more at:

http://weblog.tetradian.com/2012/11/08/methods-mechanics-approaches/

In our mining example, the mine decided to contact local experts. Rather than forcing 'Best practice' to work regardless of what was really happening, they decided to adopt new 'customised' Best practices. These were informed by small-scale experiments. By doing this they could see that although the context seemed the same for all mining, certain critical details were very different. Using local expertise had various advantages and helped inform a new 'Best practice' which was suitable for South America.

Are you ignoring low probability risk?

Mitigating risks of damage to trust

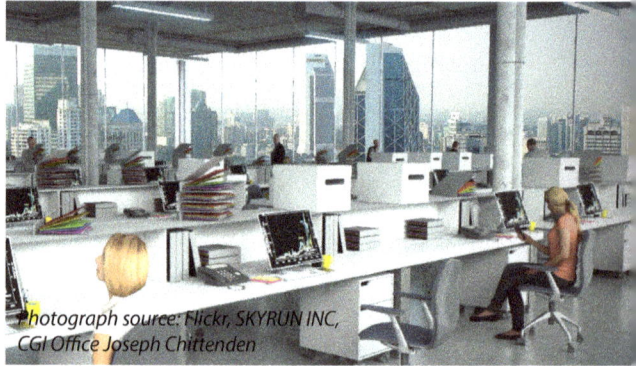
Photograph source: Flickr, SKYRUN INC,
CGI Office Joseph Chittenden

The scenario
*An investment firm had been made aware of the potential
risk of investing in a new technology, but the risk had seemed
highly unlikely and so was ignored. Years later unrelated events
started to create the perfect conditions for the potential risk to
actually happen. By this time the risk had started to magnify
into a huge problem which didn't just effect the investment firm
but entire governments. This could have been avoided by better
understanding the entire context, rather than just bits of it.*

*Are you ignoring low
probability risk?*
is based on the Tetradian
weblog post:
http://weblog.tetradian.
com/2014/04/07/playing-
pass-the-grenade/

The kurtosis-risk
Are we playing *pass the grenade* with our business? Is our
entire industry doing it? And if so, what can we do to defuse
the grenade?

In this type of context, the grenade is a metaphor for the
creation of a **kurtosis-risk** (*a seeming low-probability risk that,
when it occurs, more than wipes out all of the gains previously
made by ignoring that risk*). In business, the most common
kind of *grenade* is anything which undermines trust of that
business, whether from customers, suppliers, the market
in general, investors, or other seemingly *non-involved*
stakeholders further out in the shared-enterprise.

Some of the more infamous examples include:
• *Customer-service* whose design, either by default or by intent,
  denies those who need that service from receiving it.
• Policies and procedures that make it all but impossible to
  obtain service or self-service.
• Abuses and misuses of monopoly position or status.
• Misleading or dubious sales-practices.
• Carelessness with or cavalier attitudes to customer-data,
  privacy, or outright spying.

Pass the grenade occurs when the risk is ignored because it seems to be *(very)* low-probability, but is then increased through creation of many more instances of the same risk. Each individual instance remains a low-probability risk, such as when people become inured to poor-quality service. But the collective risk that some customer will finally scream *"I'm not going to take it any more!"* and do something about it increases with each instance. The result is what looks like a low-probability risk that is actually increasing every day, and yet it still remains all but impossible to identify which instance will be the one that finally explodes.

The risk increases even further, and grows in scale and potential impact, when an entire industry or culture joins in the game, hence *pass the grenade*. Often there is awareness that the risk is real, but hiding in denial, or in the hope that it will only be someone else, some other company, some other player, who's holding the grenade when it finally explodes. However, if the explosion is sufficiently severe to take down an entire industry, that kind of hope isn't much of a defence…

The only real way to mitigate the risk is to look at the context as a whole, to identify points where trust may be placed at risk, and mitigate those. However, these mitigations often imply apparent costs, especially in the short-term. Which means that pressures may be applied to continue to ignore the risks, on grounds of cost. These pressures will come particularly from those that assume that *low-risk* equates to *no risk*. And, perhaps even more, from stockholders who stand to gain financially from short-term profits but who are isolated and protected from the risks, or who may even take out an *each-way bet*, such that they always win, regardless of what happens to the company and to everyone else.

Loss of trust creates non-clients, or at best merely disengaged and unwilling clients. But betrayal of trust creates active anti-clients: people who have what is, to them, clear motivation to bring down the business-model of those who they feel have betrayed them. The motivation may be expressed as action against *the betrayers*, which, with the leverage now provided by social-media, may have far greater impacts than in the past. But the motivation may also be expressed as design of alternate business-models that can bypass or render irrelevant those of *the betrayers*, including bypassing apparently-unbreakable monopolies.

Trying to pretend that the problem doesn't exist, or suppress any acknowledgement of the problem, or try to force it

The Knock-on effects tool *(Book 2, page 68) can be used to explore how risk can increase when resolving an issue.*

always to be *somebody else's problem*, doesn't make the risk go away. All it does is make it worse, making a more damaging explosion even more likely. Whichever way we play it, *pass the grenade* is not a wise game to play…

Implications for enterprise-architecture

Perhaps the key role of enterprise-architecture is to ensure that, across the whole of the scope in context, **things work better when they work together, on purpose**. In turn, trust is perhaps the key lubricant for *things working together*. Without trust, everything grinds to a halt. Hence we can visualise trust, and its active counterpart of commitment, as being the centre-point around which everything in the enterprise would revolve.

In this sense, management and maintenance of trust is a fundamental concern for all forms of enterprise-architecture. The relevant forms of trust may vary somewhat according to the scope of the enterprise-architecture. In IT-only enterprise-architectures, for example, we might see trust primarily in terms of privacy, security and reliability. But whatever the context and scope, the principle remains the same: trust is at the very centre of the enterprise, and without it, nothing works.

To mitigate risks of damage to trust, we might need some or all of the following:

The Service cycle tool (Book 2, page 30) can be used to map out the stages of a service from the perspective of a customer and your organisation.

Do customer-journey mapping and customer-experience mapping to identify any trust-related issues, preferably iterative multiple-journey mapping, as trust typically rises or falls around repeat-business or full-completions of journeys *(from the customer's perspective, not just the organisation's)*.

The Holomap tool (Book 2, page 22) can be used to map out the stakeholders within an enterprise.

Do service-cycle mapping, as per the Service Cycle. The key concern here is that trust is only reaffirmed and maintained on completion of the whole cycle, including to the satisfaction of those in the *outer (non-active)* regions of the shared-enterprise, not merely the transaction-oriented subset that occurs in the more-visible middle-stages of the cycle. Similarly, and especially over the longer-term, the service-cycles need to fully encompass the strategic linkage to the shared-enterprise, as well as the tactical and operational concerns that are the more visible concern for the organisation.

Watch for any tendency in business-models, service-designs or systems-operations to fall into the classic *quick-profit failure-cycle*, where loss of connection back to the more *feeling*-oriented strategic realms also leads directly to loss of trust.

Trust is fundamental here: and the *quick-profit failure-cycle* is a long-proven anti-pattern for destroying trust in a business. Despite many common business-delusions, the organisation does not *possess* the shared-enterprise *(see page 78)*, and loss of trust will lead to ejection from the shared-enterprise. Or, to put it another way: *loss of trust = loss of business = loss of all possibility for profit*.

Mitigation of this *very real* risk provides the business-reason for enterprise-architectures that focus on whole-of-context concerns such as trust, rather than the kind of domain-specific *efficiency* focus more typical of classic IT-oriented enterprise architecture.

In addition to customer-experience mapping and service-cycle mapping:
 Do trust-mapping, to identify potential sources and leaks for trust. Probably the most useful approach is to apply conventional asset-mapping, regarding *trust in the organisation* as an organisational asset.

Once we do this, we can apply much the same kind of CRUD* analysis as for other types of assets.

Note that these processes, activities and risks may occur anywhere: in IT-architectures, for example, they can often occur in the gaps between IT-systems.

Although the mapping and analysis are much the same as for data-assets, it's essential to remember that trust is a fundamentally-different type of asset.

Whilst *information about trust* may be relatively-easy to model, it's not the same as trust itself. The latter is what we need to track, and *information about trust* is only a means to that end.

Anything which damages trust, and especially anything that does so in a way that is seemingly-easy to ignore in the short-term, is a potential *grenade*: tracking these down, and mitigating their risks, should be a core survival-concern for the organisation and its architectures.

*CRUD tasks (Create, Read, Update, and Delete) are used in computer programming as ways to work on data. A CRUD analysis explores what data should be created, read, updated and deleted, along with why, how and when.

In our investment firm example, not properly understanding the context of certain investments had led to a lack of trust amongst investors. This led to massive PR effort to try to regain that trust. Part of this effort involved looking at the long term picture, rather than their typical short term view.

How do you value people?
Working together for mutual benefit

Photograph source and CGI: Joseph Chittenden

The scenario
At a high-end resort the staff were the face of the business and the first point of contact for guests. The resort owner saw the staff as assets which could easily be replaced. This had led to high staff turnover. A new more caring owner of the resort reasoned that happy staff would represent the business better than demoralised staff. A new approach to how staff were treated was practised in the resort. This led to staff taking less sick days and offering suggestions about how to better run the resort. Staff were treated as real people, rather than numbers on a spreadsheet.

How do we value people? is based on the Tetradian weblog post: http://weblog.tetradian. com/2011/01/07/people- assets-relationships- responsibility/

People, assets, relationships and responsibility
The often well-meant phrase *"our people are our greatest asset"* is actually a very dangerous thing to say.

In enterprise architecture especially, the person should never be viewed as an *asset*: instead, it is the *relationship* with that person that is the asset, and it is a real asset to the enterprise that needs to be managed as an *asset*, much as with any other type of asset. It's clear, though, that there's a lot of confusion around this point, and a lot of understandable anger, too.

We can a take a service-oriented approach to architectures, in which everything in the enterprise is a service that is *(or should)* deliver value in terms of the vision and values of that extended-enterprise. Even the organisation as a whole can be viewed as a service in that sense*.

Many of the reasons why enterprise-related architectures, particularly business-architectures and business-models, so often get into such a mess about this will come down to two core mistakes:

- Trying to manage non-physical assets as if they're physical.
- Using a possession-based approach to assets, rather than a responsibility-based approach.

Many intellectual-property models and related business-models fail because they try to treat information as if it's physical. This is why the business-models currently preferred by much of the media industry are inherently doomed to fail. Their old models depended on physical bundling *(a physical book, a physical record, a physical seat in a physical cinema)*, but the moment their *product* becomes all-virtual *(i.e. data)* it has to operate by the rules for virtual-assets, not physical-assets.

A related example of confusion about asset-types is the whole concept of pricing or valuation. What we think of as *money* is actually a composite of virtual-asset *(numbers)* and aspirational-asset *(a belief about **worth**)*. As a virtual-asset, it is, almost by definition, infinite. Pricing, however, frequently relates to physical resources, which are *not* infinite. This mismatch leads directly to problems such as inflation, bubble-valuations and the very serious dangers of the current *financial-derivatives* markets, which have no anchor in any physical reality at all…

The same frequently applies to relational-assets, typically ignoring the real asset *(the relationship)* and instead treating the real-person as *possessed property*. Employees are treated as *(disposable) human resources*, hence that obnoxious expression, about *sweating the assets*. Whilst clients and customers are described and even derided as *consumers*, with companies fighting over the *market share* of those purported *possessions*. Nowhere in this model is much if any understanding of people as people: instead, people are regarded either as objects to be controlled, and/or as subjects that *should* place themselves as subject to the corporate will.

In essence, a possession-based model tries to split an entity into *'property'* (that which is desired, and therefore held onto, sometimes literally to death), and *'anti-property'* (that which is undesirable, and therefore dumped onto others as quickly as possible). By contrast, a responsibility-based model accepts responsibility for the entity as a whole – because at a whole-of-system level, that's the only way that works. Responsibility may and often will be transferred, but in each case it should ideally be explicit, a transfer of responsibility rather than partial *'possession'* – because again anything less than that will not work over the longer term.

* Here we use the following definitions:
– A service implements the touch-points of a function.
– A function delivers changes to assets.
– A capability acts on specific categories of assets.
– An agent is an active entity with the necessary capability, inside and/or accessed via an asset.
– An asset is a resource of any type for which the service is responsible.

Please note this is an abbreviated version of the definitions, for more about these, visit: http://weblog. tetradian.com/2011/01/07/ people-assets-relationships-responsibility/

Resources are entities that are available and that could be used and/or useful in some way. Resources become assets by taking responsibility for those assets. Resources often rapidly become 'anti-assets' – causing more harm than good to the overall enterprise – wherever someone tries to take a partial 'possession' of a resource without acknowledging full personal responsibility for every aspect of that resource. Architecturally, every resource needs an identified 'owner' who is responsible for the use of that entity as an asset – in other words, a complete architecture would include a dynamic RACI matrix* for everything that is described in that architecture.

RACI Matrix
Responsible, Accountable, Consulted and Informed. The matrix is used to describe relationships with stakeholders.

Relational-assets are usually links between real-people; aspirational-assets are typically links between a real-person and an 'idea' such as a brand, or 'belongingness' in relation to a community, a work-team or an overall enterprise. The keyword here is 'between': in effect, the asset is the responsibility of both parties, and will cease to exist if either party drops it. CRM *(customer relationship management)* systems are meaningful only if the views of both parties are maintained within the system: in most cases only the view from the organisation's side is maintained, and, worse, the other end is often viewed as a *'possessed'* object or subject – which bluntly makes the whole thing meaningless, and in many cases succeeds only in damaging the relational asset. The asset is the relationship; and the relationship only exists if both parties maintain it. That's an absolutely crucial understanding that needs to be embedded in every aspect of the enterprise-architecture.

It's slightly different with aspirational assets, because the linkage is more directional: 'to' than 'between'. Yet if the 'to' end does not exist, or is dropped, the relationship is lost: and since relational-assets are often strongly bundled with aspirational-assets (e.g. a sense of connection with a company – company-as-idea, as aspirational-asset – rather than solely a single person in that company, as relational-asset), the organisation needs to be careful to maintain those entities to which people will attach aspirational links. Hence the importance of brands and the like, in marketing to 'outsiders'; but also, very much, the importance of vision and identity in providing aspirational anchors for employees and other 'insiders'. Each of those aspirational-anchors represents a responsibility on the part of the organisation: because without that responsibility, those links will be lost. But again, those aspirational-anchors are not 'possessions' that can be bought and sold *(as in the largely delusory concept of 'goodwill' and the like)*; instead, they exist because of and as an expression of the responsibility itself.

If the responsibility is dropped, or not treated with appropriate respect, the links will dissipate rapidly – , as can be seen with many 'brand-disasters'.

The other point here is the role of relational-assets in context of the agent in a service-architecture. The agent carries and enacts the capability. We often refer to agents as *'assets'*, but in reality all agents are connected to the service via relational-links of some kind. Where the agent is a physical machine or an IT system, the relational-link is embedded in configuration – the physical and/or virtual placement of the agent and its capability within within a system. A *'configuration management database' (CMDB)* is actually a record of relational links of assignment: the active-resource (machine or IT-system) is viewed as an *'asset'*, although that term should really apply only to the static physical and/or virtual entities in which the capability is embedded, not the active capability. It's the routine and largely unconscious bundling here that causes so many architectural problems.

Importantly, though, a computer is not capable of taking responsibility, or expressing choice in its assignment *('configuration')*: that's one of the reasons why it's so easy to ignore the relational-asset in this context. However, real-people do have the ability to take responsibility, and do have choice – and hence the relational-asset needs to be explicit in the architecture. Hence, in turn, the crucial point that although the requisite capability is embedded in that real-person, in terms of how that capability is linked into a service it is the relationship that is the asset, not the person. Architecturally, the skills and responsibilities of real-people should never be embedded directly in the architecture:
– They must always be linked only via an explicit relational-asset. Where human skills and competencies are involved, the available capability is determined by the strength of that relationship, the integrity of the relational-asset. And that relational-asset is the responsibility of both parties: if either side drops it, or damages it – such as via the company describing those people themselves as *'assets'* to be *'sweated'* – the available capability will be reduced, perhaps even to nothing, even though the nominal capability of that *'asset'* remains unchanged.

The key asset in each case is the relationship via which the agent is linked to the service, and hence enacts and enables the delivery of that service. Although each of these assets involves two parties, there is only one asset in each case, with matching responsibilities on both sides of the relationship.

In our resort example, the cleaners had been seen as easily replaceable faceless assets. The more caring latest owner of the resort tried doing a cleaners job to see how hard it actually was. This led to the cleaners feeling that their voices were being heard and the owner proposing high end cleaning equipment.
This benefited the cleaners and led to the resort's hygiene rating increasing, which benefited the owner and all stakeholders.

How to be more effective together?

Things work better when they work together, on purpose

CGI: Joseph Chittenden

The scenario

A wine producer in Australia worked well but sometimes work-tasks were missed or duplicated. In the past they had a 'blame culture' but shouting at each other didn't actually resolve anything. They instead decided to try to work together on purpose. This involved them examining key areas such as: How integrated were they as wine producers? They found that often they were not communicating efficiently using appropriate channels. This exploration of how they did things and why led them to work together far more effectively.

How to be more effective together?
is based on the Tetradian weblog post:
http://weblog.tetradian.com/2015/06/02/tagline-for-enterprise-effectiveness/

What is a simple tagline that we can use to help guide conversations about enhancing enterprise-effectiveness?

Some prefer this: "*Things work better when they work together, on purpose*".

Although that doesn't quite give us the full effectiveness-summary set – *efficient, reliable, elegant, appropriate, integrated* (see Book 2, page 34)).

To cover the whole of that set, the tagline would have to be quite a bit longer: "*Things work better when they work together, efficiently, reliably, simply and elegantly, on purpose*". Which is rather unwieldy, and too long for a simple tagline.

Let's strip it right down to an even shorter form – "*things work better together on-purpose*" – and explore what arises as we go word-by-word through that short-form tagline…

Things

What 'things'? What is the 'What' of the enterprise?

This is in a deliberately-blurry sense at first, such as:
- "What is happening?" Lose detail– and from there, work slowly towards specifics. There's a literal sense to this, of course – physical assets – but a broader sense too, around information, relations, brands, reputation, and more.
- What are the 'things' of this enterprise?
- Who or what decides what things are in-scope for this enterprise, and which aren't?
- What happens to those things? In what ways do they change? – become transformed into or used in other things? (And what happens to those other things?)
- What are the life-cycles for those things? – Create, Read, Update, Delete, and so on?
- Who or what decides what should or should not happen to each thing? Why?
- Who owns each of these things? In what sense of 'own'? And what stage in each life-cycle for each thing?

Another term for 'things' is assets. In effect, things or 'resources' become 'assets' when someone has responsibility for them – whether they know it or not. We also need to note that each thing or asset will express one or more of the asset-dimensions:

As a quick summary of the distinctions between these asset-dimensions: *Physical, Virtual, Relational and Aspirational* (see Book 2, page 6).

These distinctions are crucially important, and a lot of people get them mixed up. For example, trying to 'control' information as if it's physical is rarely a good idea – especially if our business-model assumes that that'll work.

Two other points to note. One is that people – business people especially – will often ask why money, for example, isn't there as a separate dimension in its own right. That's because it isn't: technically-speaking, money is just information about a belief, in other words a combination of the virtual and aspirational dimensions.

The other is that, by intent, there's no mention of people as such. That's because people are not things – and we need to hammer that point home rather hard sometimes. Yes, relations with people are a kind of 'thing'; beliefs are a kind of 'thing'; reputation is a kind of 'thing'; and yes, those are in that mapping of asset-dimensions (typically as combinations of relational-dimension and aspirational-dimension).

The Sense-making tool
(Book 2, page 10) can be used to make sense of an issue which is being addressed by an enterprise.

The Effectiveness tool
(Book 2, page 34) can be used to guide how your organisation can resolve issues more effectively.

Relations with people are assets, but people *themselves* are not – and failure to understand that distinction is a really common cause of ineffectiveness in the enterprise.

Work

What is *'work'*? What is the *'How'* of the enterprise, that we could aim to make more effective?

The challenge here is almost the opposite to that for *'things'*: it's too easy for discussions about work to become constrained to existing assumptions, whereas for this we need to keep exploration more open for as long as possible.

Some questions to play with around *'work'*:

– What is *'work'*, within the enterprise?
– What needs to be done on or to or with all of those *'things'* of the enterprise?
– Who or what does that work?
– Who decides what work is to be done? Does this differ from the person who does the work?
– Who is responsible or accountable for that work? Is such responsibility freely chosen, or assigned by another? What are the consequences for that choice?
– If the work is automated, who designs or operates that automation? Who provides oversight or checks on that design and operation of automation?

If we think of work in terms of services, then the Enterprise Canvas framework *(see Book 2, page 18)* can provide a useful visual-checklist to guide explorations about work within the enterprise:

Every element and exchange on the Enterprise Canvas frame represents some kind of work that needs to be done on some kind of *'things'*. It may be helpful to use a semi-structured method such as the *'This'* game* to guide exploration of the work, the *'things'* and their interdependencies.

*The 'This' game is a technique the author developed for collecting information about services. It is described in more detail at: http://weblog.tetradian. com/2012/06/18/using-the- this-game-in-ea-modelling/

Better

What do we mean by *'better'*? We can ask questions such as:

– What is the quality of the enterprise, such that we know when the enterprise is more effective, or less effective, in terms of its aims and goals?
– What, in terms of the overall enterprise, is *'better'* or *'not-better'*?
– How would you identify when *'better'* has or has not been achieved? What metrics or other identifiers would you use?
– Who determines the values and metrics upon which *'better'* or *'not-better'* is based?
– For which groups of stakeholders – whether *'internal'* or *' external'* – does each aspect of *'better'* or *'not-better'* apply?

Where those metrics differ between stakeholder-groups, how would you obtain and monitor appropriate balance for and between each of the stakeholder-groups?
Where those metrics and outcomes differ across various aspects or domains of the enterprise, how would you obtain and monitor appropriate balance for and between each of the domains, and across the overall enterprise as a whole?
That last pair of questions is extremely important, yet often missed – though it's where and why we so often end up with local efficiency, for example, at the expense of overall effectiveness. The old adage *"act local, think global"* definitely applies here…

One place to start is with the effectiveness-set that we have mentioned previously– *efficient, reliable, elegant, appropriate, integrated.*

We do need to recognise, though, that that's only a starter-set, one that's common to every organisation and enterprise. To go further, we need to explore all of the other qualitative *'ilities'* that might apply in the context, such as flexibility, adaptability, extensibility, scalability and so on – all of the so-misnamed *'non-functionals'* of the respective enterprise. It would also be wise to explore the often-crucial distinctions between fragility, robustness, resilience and anti-fragility that may apply in each aspect of the enterprise and its context.

together

What do we mean by *'together'*? What underpins the integration of activities and everything else in the enterprise, to work together as a unified whole?

As above with *'better'*, exploring this aspect of effectiveness can be much harder than we might expect – though in this case more often from fixed assumptions about what *'togetherness'* supposedly *'should'* be, rather than what it needs to be for things to work well. Some questions to play with around *'together'*:

What are the key interdependencies across the enterprise? *(You may well need to go quite a lot deeper than you might at first expect, though the 'Just Enough Detail' principle should always apply.)*
Who is responsible or accountable for each interdependency? *(The answer should never be 'No-one'…)*
What are the touch-points and exchanges between each of the services that make up the activities of the enterprise?
What interdependencies do each of these interfaces and exchanges create? *(Again, the 'Just Enough Detail' principle should apply here.)*

– Who is responsible and accountable for each of these interfaces and exchanges? *(Again, the answer should never be 'No-one'.)*
– What checks and balances are needed to link everything together across the enterprise in the most optimal way overall? – allowing for the dynamics of change across the enterprise?
– What conversations between stakeholders are needed across the enterprise, to ensure optimal integration and *'togetherness'* throughout the enterprise?
– Who is responsible and accountable for each of those conversations, and the outcomes of those conversations? *(Once again, the answer should never be 'No-one'.)*

As before, the Enterprise Canvas tool and the *'This'* game may well be useful to guide this kind of exploration.

One of the most common concepts for *'togetherness'* is alignment to a defined business-strategy. Whilst that's obviously an important aspect of *'togetherness'*, it's only one aspect amongst many – and if we fail to acknowledge and work with that fact, we can get ourselves into very deep trouble without understanding how or why. We need to remember at all times that the enterprise-in-scope is always larger than the organisation-in-scope:

The interdependencies, touch-points, exchanges, checks and balances, and conversations needed for *'togetherness'* apply to relations between all stakeholders in the overall enterprise – not solely to those interactions that seemingly centre around the organisation itself. Again, we forget that fact at our peril..

On-purpose

What do we mean by *'on-purpose'*? What is the *'Why'* for the enterprise, that underpins everything that it is and does?

In principle, *'on-purpose'* should be straightforward: every action in the enterprise should take place in context of a shared-purpose – sometimes described as the *'vision'* for the shared-enterprise. Every service acts as a means to move from what we already have – the *'realised-ends'* in the existing real-world – towards that vision, the *'desired-ends'*.

Yet as with *'Together'*, the real challenge here is that there are often some too-rigid preconceptions about what the *'Why'* is for an enterprise, and even more for who gets to define it – many of which preconceptions may well be dangerously wrong… So, some questions to play with around *'on-purpose'*:

- What is the purpose of the enterprise, as a central rallying-point for a 'bold endeavour'?
- How is that enterprise-purpose identified?
- Who defines that purpose? – or does it kind of define itself, for example using POSIWID* .
- What values devolve from the shared-purpose? How do these help to identify what *'better'* would mean within the enterprise, and how to keep on-track towards both *'better'* and *'on-purpose'*?
- How do we identify when actions are more towards, or less towards, *'on-purpose'*? What can we do to bring strategies and actions more towards *'on-purpose'*?
- What is the purpose or intent of each stakeholder-group in relation to that shared enterprise-purpose?
- What action needs to be taken to ensure that those differing purposes balance out in relation to each other and to the shared-purpose? How can we ensure that the purposes of one or more stakeholder-groups do not attempt to override all of the others?

It's perhaps crucial to note that every stakeholder has their own aims and purposes – many of which are changing all the time anyway. For example, a bar/restaurant chain wants to make a financial profit, the franchisee wants to run a business, the employees want meaningful work that also supports their own families, the city wants to attract visitors to the town, the police want no trouble from anyone, whilst the customer – right now, though perhaps not at any other time – just wants a good night out with something good to eat and drink. And the shared-enterprise is the point where all of these disparate purposes coincide.

Which is why, for enterprise-effectiveness, we need to understand that no-one *'possesses'* the enterprise – it is itself, it just *'is'*. And likewise no-one *'possesses'* the shared-purpose for that shared-enterprise – it is itself, it just *'is'*. To design a business-model in relation to that shared-enterprise, we need to know what that shared-purpose is – but we also need to remember that we do not define that shared-purpose, nor do we possess it. This is a crucial point that many business-folk still seemingly fail to understand…

The usual approach to business-models and the like would typically assume that the organisation *'is'* the enterprise, and that everyone else exists only in relation to the organisation and its own needs, aims and purpose. This shift in perspective about the nature of enterprise above warns us that conventional view is literally self-centric – and fundamentally wrong, causing serious misconceptions about the nature of value-propositions and the like.

In our wine producer example, they examined what was the purpose for each stakeholder and what needed to be done to balance out their needs. The grape pickers needed good working conditions while maintaining quality. Management invested in better picking equipment which helped the pickers through the working day and kept the grapes in better condition ready for processing.

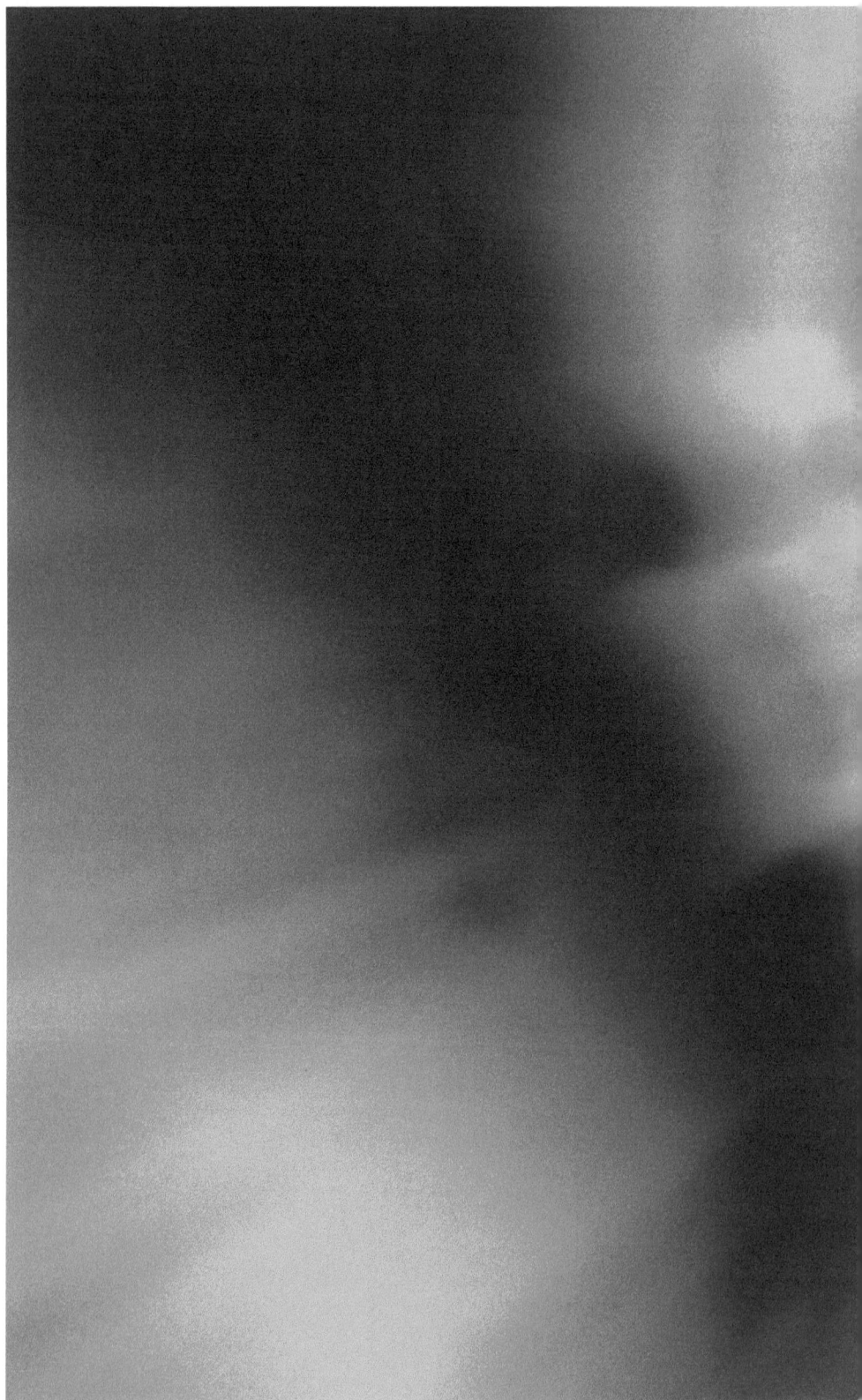

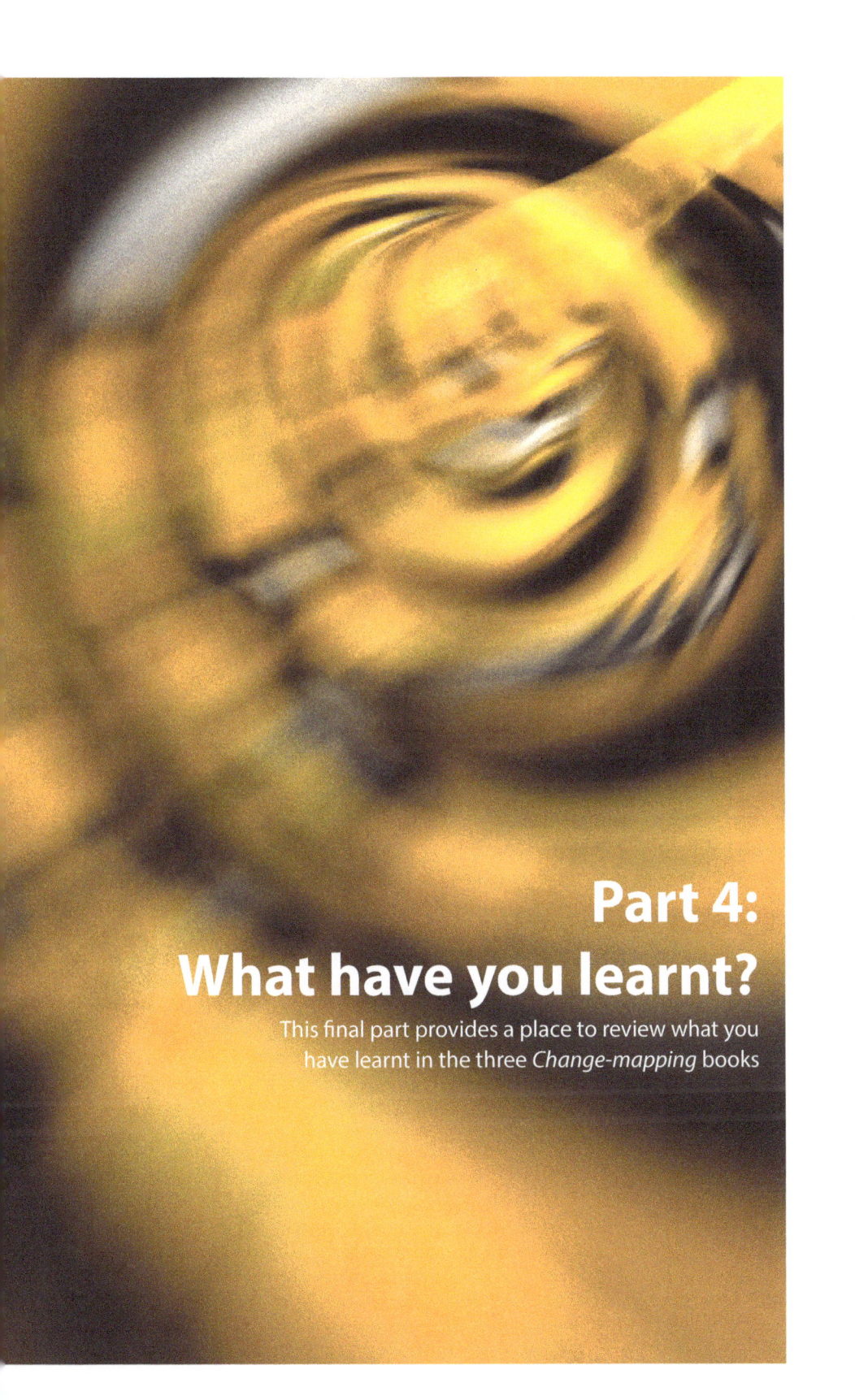

Part 4:
What have you learnt?

This final part provides a place to review what you
have learnt in the three *Change-mapping* books

What have you learnt?

A summary of *Change-mapping*

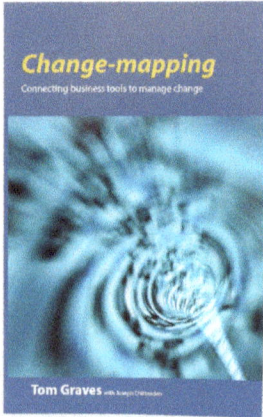

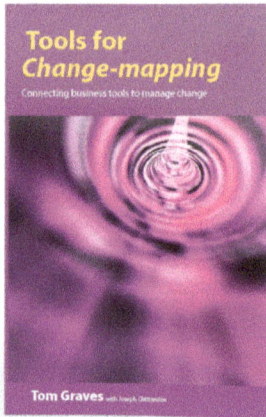

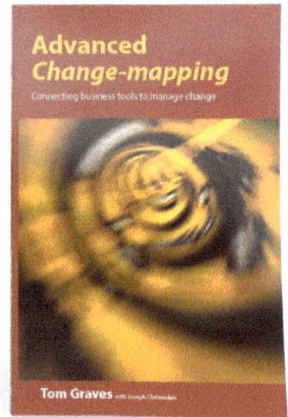

Any issue of any size

Where this all started was that the two of us - one a designer, the other an enterprise-architect - both needed some way to connect together every part of our projects. Sometimes we needed to connect things side-to-side, across departments; sometimes top-to-bottom, from strategy to operations and back again; often both directions at the same time. So many different tools and methods needed to make this work, most of which wouldn't work well with each other at all. If you're involved in guiding any kind of change, in business or elsewhere, we can guess that you've had the same troubles too.

What we needed most was a way to connect everything together, everywhere. A change-method that would work the same way with any type of content or context, for every scope and scale, any level of complexity, every part of a change. A method to help us do the right things right, adapt itself to any size of project, and help us keep track of everything that we did. We called it *Change-mapping*.

We've made it as simple as possible, so that anyone can learn it. And as you'll have seen, we've split the material across three books, to make it easier for everyone to learn.

Book 1: *Change-mapping*

In the first book, we introduced the core concepts for *Change-mapping*, such as the way that every mission starts from an *issue*, a request for some kind of change. We showed you the *five main types of task* within a mission - Context, Scope, Plan, Action and Review - and why they rely on that sequence to make everything work. We described the different *roles*, such as Pathfinder, Observer, and the Explorers. And we included some basic pre-packaged *tools* to go with each of the tasks, to give you enough to get started on some practice with real-world missions.

Book 2: *Tools for Change-mapping*

In the second book, we showed you how to extend the capabilities of your *Change-mapping*, introducing the core concept of tools as *'plug-ins'*. This makes it possible for you to plug in any almost tool or technique that may be needed. Combining this with *nesting* - doing a 'mini-mission' inside the current mission - makes it simple to drill down into any level of the detail for an issue that you might need, all whilst still using the same *Change-mapping* methods to connect everything together. To help you explore how this works in practice, we provided a further twenty ready-made tools to use in tasks for Context or big-picture, for Scope or people-related, and for Plan. We also provided some example missions in which to apply these and other tools.

Book 3: *Advanced Change-mapping*

In this third book, we add the final core concept for *Change-mapping*: the idea of *linked-missions*, in which linking missions together in a chain, a loop, a set of branches, or some other sequence will make it straightforward for you to tackle change-projects of any size or complexity. As you've seen, we provided a full worked-example of this as the main part of the book.

For larger projects, you may need extra *roles*, such as the Coordinator or Librarian, or extra *facilities*, such as the Library. In this book, we've described all of these, and when and how to use them.

Yet whatever the scope or scale, whatever the content or context, whatever the level of complexity, and whatever plug-in tools you use, the core principles and practices of *Change-mapping* will always remain exactly the same. As you gain more practice and experience with it, that power and simplicity of *Change-mapping* will show its real value more and more each day.

What's next?

To build your skills in *Change-mapping*, what you'll need most is real-world practice. For example, we would recommend running an **Enterprise mission** *(see page 66)*, because this will provide a good introduction to running a larger *Change-mapping* mission, yet without the pressures of time. The outcomes will usually be immediately useful for your own organisation, and it will also help you to see the benefits of understanding the big-picture, which will filter down to any project you work on later on.

Also essential is to gain practice at testing your results as you go. To do this with *Change-mapping*, always make sure to check the **Learning deliverables** *(see page 76)* from each mission: for example, these can be enormously useful when trying to rebuild a long forgotten project from the past.

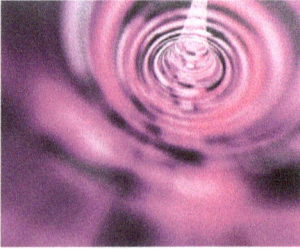

The covers on this series of the book try to show the 'rabbit-hole'.

Build the discipline

Tackling large projects demands a lot of discipline. *Change-mapping* can help a lot with that. For example, take the old adage *'Do the right things; Do things right'*: Context and Scope will help to clarify *'Do the right things'*, Plan and Action will help with *'Do things right'*, and Review will help to check that the right things were done right, and learn how to do better each time.

We also often use another guideline: *'I don't know; it depends; just enough detail'*. First, accept that you don't know, and that you need to explore; then look for the connections, the dependencies; then dive down to the right level of detail - not too little, not too much, but just the right amount. Getting that last part right can take practice, but you'll find that *Change-mapping* will help with that.

Bridging the gap

Systems thinking is a way of making sense of the complexity of the world by looking at it in terms of wholes and relationships rather than by splitting it down into its parts. Wikipedia

To tackle complex issues in change-projects, you will likely find real value from combining *Change-mapping* with insights from systems-thinking* and whole-enterprise architectures. We've introduced you to some of the latter in Part 3 of this book, where we used essays from the Tetradian weblog to highlight some unexpected traps and challenges that can be 'hiding in plain sight' even within some of the most simple-seeming business-concerns. Along with the weblog mentioned above, Tetradian have published many books and other resources to help you bridge the gap between the practice-focus of *Change-mapping* and those other more theory-based approaches to complex large-scale change.

the Tetradian weblogs

Creating a career
in Enterprise Architecture

Theory, roles and practice

Tom Graves

Further resources

Visit the *Change-mapping* section of the Tetradian website at *http://tetradian.com* for new tools, templates and other resources.

The Tetradian weblog at *http://weblog.tetradian.com* has more than a thousand posts on systems-thinking, enterprise-architecture and more. Anthologies from the weblog content, such as the ***Creating a career in enterprise-architecture*** anthology shown above, are published in ebook formats at *https://leanpub.com/u/tetradian* , where you'll also find ebooks from the **Tetradian on Enterprise-Architecture** series. Finally, do explore the Tetradian channel on YouTube, at *https://www.youtube.com/user/tetradian* . There are already almost two hundred videos there, on *'Tools for change'* and more, with further videos added often.

www.ingramcontent.com/pod-product-compliance
Lightning Source LLC
Chambersburg PA
CBHW042118190326
41519CB00030B/7534